GW01090298

REFLECTIONS
ON
ASCENSION

CHANNELED
TEACHINGS
OF ST. FRANCIS

by
ANINA DAVENPORT

Published by
OUGHTEN HOUSE PUBLICATIONS
LIVERMORE, CA USA

Reflections on Ascension: Channeled Teachings of St. Francis
by
Anina Davenport

Published in 1998
Copyright © 1998 Anina Davenport

00 99 98   0 9 8 7 6 5 4 3 2 1

Please note that nothing in this book is meant to keep you from seeking advice. If you are suffering from any of the symptoms described herein, you are advised to see a physician.

Published by
OUGHTEN HOUSE PUBLICATIONS
PO BOX 2008
LIVERMORE, CA 94551
PHONE: (510) 447-2332
FAX: (510) 447-2376
E-MAIL: oughten@oughtenhouse.com
INTERNET: www.oughtenhouse.com

Library of Congress Cataloging in Publication

Francis, of Assisi, Saint, 1182 - 1226 (Spirit)
    Reflections on ascension : channeled teachings by St. Francis /
by Anina Davenport
        p. cm.
        ISBN 1-880666-71-5
        1. Spirit Writings. 2. Ascension Day--Miscellanea
    I. Davenport, Anina, 1961 –   II. Title
    BF1311.F67F73   1997
    133.9'3--DC21

                                        97-33184
ISBN 1-880666-71-5   CIP
Printed in the USA

Contents

Acknowledgments

Thank you to my **husband** for his unconditional love and acceptance.

To **Hannah** for spreading your joy.

To **Mary** for being the best friend one could ever ask for.

To **Jane** for constantly reminding me that I have choices.

To **Sallie** for being a true sister.

To **Susan** for your wisdom and help with the book.

To **Brian** for your support.

To **St. Francis** for your wisdom, love and sense of humor.

To my **mother** for her love, compassion and courage.

To my **father** for being a role model on how to swim against the stream.

To **Joy** and **Tony** and all the other people at Oughten House for their support.

To all those who I have not mentioned by name. I have been supported in so many ways.

To all the light workers. I believe we all work together and open doors for each other.

Introduction by St. Francis

This book is a series of channeled teachings and explorations on the ascension process. The channel was so kind to serve as a mouthpiece for our concepts and ideas and she decided to add some of her own thoughts.

As many of you are aware, there are new energies and frequencies that have recently entered this planet and we—as your guides, or friends as we prefer to be called—are very pleased with the accomplishments of this "project" which many call ascension. It is a mighty project, indeed, and many intelligences or energies are involved in the co-creation of this magnificent undertaking.

You, dear readers, are very much involved in this undertaking and this is one of the points that we would like to get across in this book. You are, in a way, the ground troops and although we do not particularly like military language, there is an appropriate analogy here. Like ground troops, you are in the midst of a "battle" and that is more about holding the light than anything else.

Most of you are constantly bombarded by the misunderstandings and confusion of the so-called "real world." Being told that the problems and desires of the ego are, in the final analysis, just an illusion is not always helpful. Or, to quote our dear channel after being reminded of the illusory quality of one of her "problems," "Easy for you to say." And we concur laughingly, lovingly, and with compassion. It is not always easy holding on to your light and remembering that all that really counts is your I AM Presence, your awareness of your Oneness with God, with All That Is.

This world of distractions and thought systems that constantly tells you that you are not good enough, not whole and complete, and that you cannot be happy without this car, house, soul-mate or whatever else it is that is being "sold" to you, will probably feel more and more insane to you as you continue on the path of ascension.

vi • Reflections on Ascension

This is not to say that there is anything wrong with having a car or a house or a fulfilling job. We want all of you to have fun and enjoy yourselves, but please ask why you have the car. Do you have a car because you have a car, or do you have a car because deep down inside you believe you are not complete without a car, a husband, a wife, a career, a meditation practice, a specific workshop, an ascension tape? Whatever it is, your ego can use it.

Let us add that we are not here to frighten the ego. In our perspective—and others have different points of view—the ego is a bit like a lost child that has just been given the control of the family. The ego is basically made up of fear. The more the ego realizes that this ascension path is a "good thing," the more it will relax, and the energy that is caught up in this strange energy gestalt called ego will be set free to transform back into the light that it once was. Nothing ever gets lost in this universe and whatever energy you offer to us, or more appropriately your own Self, including your Higher Self, will be used to serve the Divine Plan.

Let us try to explain who we are. "Try" is the operative word here, because words are not adequate to describe who we are or, for that matter, who you (the reader) are, behind that little facade called personality. All of you are part of a magnificent Being and your personality is only the very tip of this incredible energy gestalt that you are a part of—or more accurately, that you are.

We would encourage you to investigate and explore more of who you are because that will allow you to understand more of who we are. And we will repeat ourselves in telling all of you that we are really all One. You do not have to believe this, but maybe you could take the possibility into consideration.

So let us try again. We are part of a beautiful, magnificent energy gestalt much as you are. The difference between some of you and us is that we are more aware of it. Now, we are not completely aware of all that we are. In fact that is the purpose of evolution—to continuously discover and explore more of who you are.

We are connected to the energy called Kuthumi. In fact we are part of this energy gestalt. Some might call us an aspect. We have chosen the name St. Francis for our channeling primarily because this channel knew us as St. Francis in Assisi and trusts us (with this name). St. Francis is, of course, just the aspect that is at the forefront of this Being (in this particular channeling). We are so much more than St. Francis. "Technically" (laughing), we are not even St. Francis any more—that is the "old St. Francis" who had a lot of limiting beliefs. You see, death is not the end and everybody continues to evolve, including so-called "saints."

We will talk more about who we are throughout this book. Indeed, we will repeat certain concepts periodically. As you might know, learning occurs in a circular/spiral manner rather than a straight line. This means that concepts need to be repeated at different times on the "learning spiral." In truth, life is very much like a spiral and the idea of progress as a straight line is a distortion of your time-space "set-up." Consciousness uses that distortion when you need to focus on details, but when looking at life itself the concept of a spiral is more helpful.

One of the subjects we will be talking about is discernment. As you know, not all channeling is well intentioned or particularly accurate. So we ask you to always examine anything you hear or read.

You are the gatekeepers of your beliefs and you decide what you will let in and what rings true to you. We know that deep inside, you know what is right for you. So how about this book? Is it worth reading? Is it true for you, or is at least some of it relevant for you? You decide. You are the creator of your own experience.

We offer these concepts and understandings with love. You know, it gives us great pleasure to connect with you and we truly marvel at your creatorship.

Introduction by Anina

I first heard about the concept of ascension when I visited a healing circle to help me heal a sprained ankle. At first I did not know what people were talking about. I had read a lot of spiritual books and was very interested in the concept of enlightenment, but ascension—what was that? Was it like enlightenment or was it different? Was it something good? Was it just something Jesus did and we should not really mention such a lofty word in regard to ourselves? And what did Jesus do anyway? How does it all work?

Well, you can tell I was intrigued. I continued going to the healing circle and to classes held by the woman leading the circle. There was much I did not understand, but my ankle got better and I could feel some energy heating up my body. Weak circulation and chronically cold feet had changed into healthy looking skin and hot feet. At times my hands would become so warm that my husband named me "Mrs. Hot Hands."

Still wondering what was happening, I continued to go to the healing circles and began to read books on ascension. Then I felt the impulse to do a lot of writing. I had always been aware that there was a presence with me and I used to ask this presence questions by writing them down. This presence has always been loving and wise, although I could not always hear it clearly. Now words just tumbled out of me. As if a dam had been broken I wrote, wrote and wrote.

I started seeing things with my inner eyes. For example, in one healing circle one of the healers worked with me and suddenly I saw us as American Indians sitting together in a circle. I later told her about my vision and she looked startled. She is clairvoyant and had seen exactly the same picture. This was one of many wonderful confirmations. I later engaged in private sessions with this healer and asked who it was who was constantly talking to me. A guide? An angel? I knew the presence was too loving to be "evil."

She tuned in and smiled. "St. Francis," she said.

"Who is he?" I asked, surprised. Later I headed for the library.

Since then much time has gone by and I have had numerous dreams and healing adventures with St. Francis. At some point I visited Assisi, Italy, and remembered clearly that I was a monk during his time there.

In the larger picture, our relationship is still a bit of a mystery to me. Let me share with you the puzzle pieces that I do have. I know that I am part of the St. Francis entity and that, in a way, he is connected to my Higher Self. In my experience, the St. Francis energy is very much one of love, calm, and peace. This is also very much my energy—that is, when I am centered and not "con-fused" with other energies. St. Francis once gave me the image of the turtle—slow, steady and peaceful. Another picture he once presented of my basic energy was that of a cello in an orchestra.

I will talk more about the idea of being related to a certain energy throughout the book. I believe it is very helpful to find out if one's energy is more akin to, let us say, a triangle or a trumpet. This helps us more easily understand how we need to move along in the physical world, what makes us happy, and how we can best serve the Divine Plan.

In one dream, St. Francis showed me that he also has a Higher Self, and he is still learning just the as we are learning. Ultimately, of course, we are all connected. On the highest level we are all One—One with Source, One with All That Is.

As time went by I did more and more channeling, and gave free and informal readings for friends. I also received many readings from a dear friend who had just begun channeling as well. Looking back, I see now that I did a lot of belief system work. I let go of a lot of old limiting beliefs and learned to allow a more loving truth to resurface.

As I engaged in channeling, the energy experiences continued. For me that meant a lot of heat and other phenomena. Some nights I could hear little beeping noises that reminded me of Morse Code signals. My guides used such "toning" to crack the energy forms of the old beliefs I was releasing. At times I could see the energy in the room dancing and changing. Other times I saw colors. I was often tired and felt as is my whole body was being reconstructed.

My response to all of this varied from excitement and joy about this wonderful adventure to simple frustration about being tired so much and about other aches and pains that seemed to be related to this process.

In March, 1995, my guides urged me to go to a seminar in Basel, Switzerland to be held by a man named Brian Grattan. He was teaching about ascension and, as I soon found out, emitting a tremendous amount of light. It was a wonderful experience and teaching. I had never met anybody so enlightened and so human at the same time. I liked Brian right away, especially because he was so human. In my opinion there was nothing fake about him. He did not pretend to be better than any of us, and at the same time he did not deny his divinity. He just said, "Look, we are all one and the same. We all come from God, Source. We are all Divine."

Little did I know—or should I say that the little "I," the personality, did not know—that Brian would leave us on the last day of the seminar. He died on Easter Monday, 1995, and up until the last day he gave of his love and compassion. After his death I had several dreams about him, and at times I heard his voice and felt his presence.

Brian Grattan has written a wonderful book called *Mahatma I & II* (Light Technology Publishing). There are also tapes available of his meditations. *Mahatma I & II* is a very powerful book and sometimes my hands get hot just from holding it. I will share some of my experiences with Brian and the Mahatma energy.

My book consists of channelings by St. Francis, and I have added some of my own experiences. Besides some "brilliant thoughts" about ascension and the universe from my friends, I wanted to bring in some of the nitty gritty of the ascension process. Maybe the channel wanted to have her say too, as in: "Yes, I know we are creating a new world but my body aches now and there are so few people to talk to." Or, "What do I do when all my "stuff" comes up?"

So you can tell that my input is very much about straddling two worlds: The one of ascension, unlimited opportunities, filling our hearts with love and unconditional acceptance and the one where somebody cuts us off at the traffic light because we waited two seconds too long. How do you live in both worlds? I understand the vision, the greater picture, but how do you actually live it? That is a constant question that I have for my guides and that is my contribution to this book.

A lot of information is from personal channelings, actual happenings and from informal readings I gave for friends. To protect their privacy, I have changed their names.

And last but not least, I want to send you, the reader, my love and regards. I believe we are all co-creating this new reality together and it is not always easy. Nevertheless, we had the courage to come here and all of us are equally important in this grand project called ascension, no matter what our specific function. It is not always apparent to the personality how we contribute and sometimes, when it seems as though nothing is happening, little light explosions are going off on many levels of our Being.

How This Book Came About

For one year I sat down every morning and began writing. Sometimes St. Francis came through with a subject that he wanted to talk about and sometimes I asked him certain questions.

I often had dreams about certain topics that I was thinking about and I later discussed these with him. Also, people would pop into my life with questions similar to the ones I had raised. Often friends of mine would wonder about the same issues.

At times I gave readings to friends and recorded sections of the channelings that I found to be of general value. Anyway, fifty notebooks later St. Francis said: "It is time to get organized."

"How?" I exclaimed, feeling overwhelmed by the sheer idea of putting all these notebooks together to a meaningful message.

"Step by step," St. Francis replied, and promised to guide me through. First he asked me to number the pages of my notebooks and then to make summaries of the topics on the back. Then I made a list of all the topics that I wanted in the book and circled them on my notebook summaries. Next he told me to buy two big folders with dividers, to cut out the topics I wanted and to put them into some kind of order. Suddenly it began to look more like a book.

St. Francis told me not to worry about some of the repetitions and commented that they served a purpose.

I share this process to let you know how the book came about and to give an example of how "grounded" and practical St. Francis can be. He has helped me greatly in many ways, not just with "lofty" spiritual concepts but also with dealing with everyday living. He helped me to slow down, to be more organized, and—this might sound funny—by following St. Francis' guidance I have even become a better driver.

1

Ascension

St. Francis:

Ascension is basically the raising of frequency. This will happen naturally and is, as we have told our channel, "our job." We, and many other energies and intelligences, are constantly sending high frequency energy to you, the Earth, plants, animals and any consciousness that has decided to ascend. On a higher level, all of you have decided to raise frequency and accelerate your growth.

Ascension is, simply put, an acceleration in vibration. We like to keep it simple because it is. There is nothing magical about it and you do not have to join some "special club" to participate. In fact, the best way for the personality to help your guides and other levels of your Self is to *relax*. Physical, mental, and "emotional" relaxation literally creates space for those other energies (which are not really "other") to come in.

You see, on another level of your Being, you are already ascended and vibrating at a higher frequency. In a way you are not creating a lightbody via this ascension process, you are trying to merge with the one you already have.

Now we, as guides, will never give you more than you can handle. Trust your Higher Self. Trust your guides. They know you intimately, and they know their purpose and their function. Remember we do not have to struggle with the kind of veils you have on Earth.

The "trick" in this ascension process is, the way we see it, the light *integration*. Therefore, we will spend a lot of time on such concepts as clearing, grounding, and generally being good to yourself while you are going through this incredible transformation process. This is especially so for the physical body, which is the densest of all the bodies (meaning physical, spiritual, emotional and mental bodies), which is asked to perform quite a "miracle," if we may use this word.

Let us comment on a question we are often asked: Why ascension? And why now? First of all, let us state that it is really a joyful event and a great gift from your Self to yourself. The Mahatma energy, or the part of Source that is accessible, has been fully anchored on Earth and great opportunities lie ahead. You — on higher levels — had decided that it is time to come back into alignment with God and ascension is one way to do this. Earth herself, this wondrous planet, has decided that she is done with this level of density and is ascending as well.

Those on Earth who do not like the fast pace of this development will find other planets to continue their evolution in their own time. However, staying on Earth *now* means accelerating evolution and nobody on this planet is excluded. It is not possible to be bombarded by high frequency energies from intelligences throughout this universe and others and not be affected. *Everybody is affected.* Not everybody realizes the joyous opportunity for growth and expansion that we have all been given in this project.

Yesterday our channel watched a television program on prophecies. The word that caught her attention was "purification." Many visionaries talked about purification and many connected it with catastrophes such as fires, earthquakes, floods and other disasters. Well, we say to you that ascension, on one level, is also a purification. Part of the ascension experience is about clearing the old—old thought patterns, old energies, old fears. Many catastrophes seen by so called visionaries will not happen, and need not happen, if consciousness is raised by raising frequency.

Anina:

The whole process is still a mystery to me but I would like to share some of the information that I have received. A couple of years ago I had a dream where somebody said to me, "God wants you all to go back to your high frequency."

As I woke up I had an understanding that at some point in time (or out of time) all of us were vibrating at a high frequency and then lowered it, probably as we entered lower densities. Later we became confused with the dense energies. I also had a sense that we could now raise frequency and stay on Earth (although some might choose to leave).

I would like to share another dream/experience. One night I came in touch with one of my past lives. I was an Indian woman living a very simple life with a husband, his mother, and his sister in a small hut in the mountains. My life consisted of gathering food, cooking, and cleaning. In the dream I was told that this life was a preparation for my ascension experience and that all my "past lives" were in some way geared to ascension. In a way, the life I live now is a culmination of all the other lives' efforts.

I think that in the life in India, I learned patience and to go slowly. There was also something important about being in the mountains, walking every day, and being grounded.

I called this dream a "dream/experience" because when I awoke, it took me quite a while to come back to this life. The other life had seemed so real and I understood my guides' comment that "past lives" are really happening right now.

This dream, and others I have had, keep reminding me that transformation is taking place on many different levels. As we heal this life, we also heal our "past lives."

Another time I dreamed that I was channeling information in many dimensions simultaneously. It is hard to
describe this dream in words but I was again shown that
life is multi-leveled, multi-dimensional, if you will, and
that we are so much more than the personality can understand.

I mention these experiences because for me, one of the
biggest challenges in the ascension process has been to
trust and not get too scared if my personality cannot understand it all. Our small mind, which works so beautifully
when we use it to drive a car, pay bills, or build a house,
can only understand so much about the ascension experience. We need to trust our Higher Self in this process.

2
Channeling

St. Francis:

Much has been written about the phenomenon called channeling. We would like to comment on the energy that is being brought through by a channel clear enough to receive the words of a higher vibration.

As you read this book you will look at certain ideas and concepts and, if they feel right to you, accept them. As you take in these ideas, you will take in certain vibrations which will resonate in your Being and strengthen concepts of relative truth that you already have.

In a way, we are not telling you anything new. By connecting with you through these words which hold a certain energy, we are just helping you to release these concepts in your Being. On a higher (and we do not quite like the word higher but it is the best we have right now) level you are very aware of these "new" ideas.

Let us go even further: On a higher level of your Being we are One, and you have co-authored this book.

A couple of years ago our channel had a dream in which she opened a book she had channeled. On the margins of the book were drawings depicting the "authors" of certain sections. She was surprised to see all kinds of energies, including owls, plants, and other conscious-nesses. She created this dream from a higher level of herself to teach herself that many consciousnesses are involved.

So, after we have probably confused you, dear reader, we suggest you let it go. Your brain might not understand but your Being does.

Anina:

As I start channeling, I feel an energy surge in my body. It seems as if I hear an inner voice and I speak fairly quickly. However, tuning in more closely, it feels more as if I am receiving energy containing certain concepts and ideas that are then quickly translated by my brain into words. During readings I get a sense of what St. Francis is trying to say, and at times I observe that certain concepts are hard to describe in third dimension. For example, when he talks about enlightenment, I always feel the inadequacy of words to describe this concept.

St. Francis has told me that no channeling is a hundred percent accurate. First, you have the distortion of putting pretty unlimited concepts into the third dimension. Secondly, the guides have to go through a channel with a personality who has his or her own beliefs about the nature of reality.

Most distortions are not conscious. I believe—or at least want to believe—that most channels want to bring through their guides' messages as purely as possible. However, if a personality has a "stake" in a certain belief, it is very possible that they are not willing to let a "contrary" statement come through. I personally do not believe channels who purport their message is a hundred percent pure. I have talked to many wonderful channels who feel the same way.

This brings us to the question of whether there is "perfection" in this physical dimension. My guides have told me that there is no perfection on Earth. I believe this Earth plane is more about learning and evolving than "becoming perfect." Going a step further, I am told that evolution itself never stops. So how can anybody or anything ever be perfect, except maybe in this very moment exactly the way it is?

Coming back to channeling and channels, the most helpful feature for me has been that channeling helps me to expand my consciousness and to let go of limiting beliefs. When I channel, I usually feel a lot of energy coming through me and my body heats up. Channeling, of course, supports my ascension process and I love the feeling of more energy being pumped through my body. A couple of hours later I am usually tired though, and sometimes my joints ache from the increased input. I trust my guides not to give me more than I can handle.

A wonderful aspect of giving readings for others is that I can feel St. Francis' love for that person. It is sometimes amazing for me to watch how the personality Anina reacts to certain questions and statements while St. Francis, in undeviating patience, keeps on explaining the same concepts over and over again.

From what I can feel while in channel, St. Francis has incredible love for everybody who comes and has genuine respect for our journeys. He sees people as magnificent creators and powerful spiritual beings. This sense of our power and courage for coming to Earth—this sometimes very tough school—is constant. Even as people continue to proclaim how unworthy and powerless they are, St. Francis will patiently listen and help them to accept the part of them that feels that way. And yet he will never agree with this point of view.

In a way, he perceives us as the powerful spiritual Beings that we are *and* he understands the pain, tribulations and joys of being in a human body. It is interesting for me to watch how he holds this vision of divinity for a person while the personality, Anina, is getting to a point of agreeing with the person that the world is horrible, that they are victims, and that there is not much they can do about it. You can tell I learn a lot from him—or should I say them—since St. Francis sees himself as part of a larger consciousness and usually uses the pronoun "we."

St. Francis has a wonderful sense of humor and he told me early on that he was teaching *en-lighten-ment* and not en-heavy-ment. When I started this book, I first tried to add verbs such as "laughing" or "amused" to give the reader a sense of the lightness and humor behind the words. I soon realized that I would have to add such verbs to almost every sentence and decided to do so very sparingly. I imagine that you, the reader, can tune in and connect with the energy behind the words and get a sense of its lightness.

3

The Higher Self Connection

St Francis:

First of all, let us say that it is natural to have a strong connection to your Higher Self. After all, you *are* your Higher Self and your Higher Self is you. In truth, there is no separation. However, in this world of illusion and separation it has become "normal" to feel confused and not know where one is going, who to listen to and how any of you fit into the greater Divine Plan.

So, you have all come to heal that separation between you the personality and your Higher Self, and from there you continue connecting with other levels of Self. Ultimately you become aware of your own connection to Source and that you are One with God. How do you get to this? Do not worry, for your Higher Self will lead you, step by step. It will show you the path, what obstacles there are to clear, and which energies (such as books, groups or teachers) can help you do so.

How do you connect to your Higher Self? Of course all of you have done so at times, but to deepen and expand this connection is, from what we see, so very, very important now.

First of all you have to *want* to connect to your Higher Self. Many have said to us, "Oh, St. Francis, we want to connect to our Higher Self but we do not seem to be able to." Our answer often has been, "Do you really want to? Yes, we can see clearly there is a part of you that wants to, but there is another part that says: No way will I follow anybody, not even my Higher Self."

Often we have heard people say, "Oh, why do I not have wonderful dreams? Why does my soul not speak to me?" And each person was sincere in his or her desire, but when lying in bed at night there is a big sign at the door that says, "Do not intrude. I do not care if you are a master, an angel or my Higher Self. Do not come in. I want to be in total control."

Now, there is nothing wrong with this voice. It surely has fulfilled a purpose at one time, but the "Do not come near me" signs make it hard for any energy to come through.

So where do you go from here? As always, always, always, you love yourself. You love all parts of yourself, including the part that seems to keep you from receiving love from other parts of your greater Self. There are many ways to love all parts of yourself and in this book we give various suggestions. The important thing is that you let *all parts of yourself* express themselves—through movement, toning, writing, talking in dreams, or whatever other way is appropriate at the time. We will talk more about this in the chapter on subpersonalities.

Let us assure you that once you unite your energies (and your subpersonalities are part of your energies), then they can support the goals of your Higher Self or your greater Self rather than obstruct your purpose and function.

Another appropriate means is prayer. Do not give up. Talk to your guides, your Higher Self, and, most important of all, talk to God or Source or the Divine or the Great Spirit or whatever label you wish to use. Labels do not matter. When you pray, what you really do is state an intent such as, "God, I really want to hear from you," or "Higher Self, please talk to me." Praying together with, talking to your many selves is, in our opinion, always successful.

4

Unconditional Acceptance

St. Francis:

There are many paths to freedom. There is confrontation and there is shock, and some personalities benefit from such methods. Ultimately, however, you will need to accept yourself unconditionally. It is this acceptance that will transform any false beliefs and energy patterns that no longer serve you.

You see, ultimately you are energy or, more precisely, energy with intent. The intent is unconditional acceptance and love, because that is what your Father/Mother/All That Is is. That is your Source—unconditional love. So how could you ever be anything else?

Ultimately, even those you call murderers or abusers are energies of unconditional love—confused maybe, but no less dear to All That Is than any of us. And be happy, because most of us have committed some so called despicable acts in our many lives. It was all part of the drama. You are no more guilty of anything than an actor who gives a brilliant performance.

This does not mean that, within the drama, action does not have consequences. The true consequence, however, comes from *self*-judgment about an act committed either in a "past" or present life. In a way, judgment was the cause of the violent act and it soon comes full circle.

If you want to stop re-cycling you need to release judgment. So, a big part of this book will be about self-acceptance and what our channel calls "the nitty gritty of it." She has asked us to be specific and we will discuss in detail so-called subpersonalities, the allowance of feelings and acceptance of your physical vehicle known as the body. We intend to express our love for the magnificent vehicle you all share on Earth and we want to say clearly that that is what it is—a vehicle.

Many of you have deep fears of getting stuck in the body because that is exactly what happened to many of you. You got trapped in the flesh and forgot how to get out. For some of you, this experience was thousands of years ago, for others much longer. Spirit trapped in matter: A frightening thought for many of you. Allow that fear—it will inform you. Write down your thoughts on this, if you wish.

Many of you started blaming the body at that point in time. It is time to express that blame and then gently release it. The body is waiting to become your ally in this journey of ascension. Your body is ready to be "spiritualized," to be infused with light. What a glorious journey it is and we are all participating

5

Divine Equality

St. Francis:

Let us make it very clear that there is divine equality in this universe and in others. Source recognizes you all as its children and there is no judgment on your evolution. As a tulip is no more dear than a rose to the devoted gardener, so Source recognizes your inherent divinity and cannot even see what you have termed "faults."

The fundamental law of divine equality is not very well understood on Earth. Ideas of better than or more powerful, of control and competition, are all part of the illusion that has been created on this beautiful planet of love and learning. The earlier you can detach yourself from the madness of concepts of inequality, lack, and "not good enough," the better. We describe in this book various methods to help you do so.

Accept yourself unconditionally in the midst of judgment, fear, feelings of control or victimization. Accept, accept, accept. This is what we see as the most efficient, the most elegant way. Living in the midst of judgment and concepts of control and powerlessness gives all of you a wonderful opportunity to heal such thoughts, not only for yourselves but also for others who, on the "highest" level are, of course, you as well.

You do not need to run away from conflict unless your Higher Self tells you to do so (sometimes that is a smart option). But generally, you can face conflict lovingly and gently by loving all parts inside yourself that believe they are in conflict; they are not really. They can coexist very well together. We will explain more later on.

So, just as you are no better than your neighbor and vice versa, so are we, the energy gestalt that we have termed St. Francis, no better. We have, maybe, a different point of view. We are not encased in the physical vehicle as some of you are, although aspects of our greater Being walk around on Earth. This channel is one of these aspects. We imagine that some of you who read this book are also aspects of our greater Being, or part of our soul group. It does not really matter. Whatever your "mothership," all of you are part of marvelous Beings. The trick is just to become more aware of those parts of you that are called by some the Higher Self, the Oversoul, the Monad and, of course, Source itself. At the root, all of you are connected. Ultimately, all of you are part of Source and Divine. So how can there be anything other than divine equality?

Beware of teachers telling you that you are less than, or not as evolved as—and most of all—that you cannot understand your greater Self. What a ridiculous idea that somehow you cannot have access to your own Self. Even this book is not necessary; you could live on a desert island and still find out everything about your greater Self that you wish to find out.

But if you enjoy conversation and our company—and we certainly enjoy yours—then please accept our invitation to merge with our energies and play with our ideas and concepts. We can be wonderful friends—our channel has found that out. We are always available to our friends on Earth and, if we may say so, we have a good sense of humor. After all, it is en-lighten-ment that we teach, not en-heavy-ment.

We invite you all to open to your Higher Self. It loves you unconditionally and appreciates all the work you are doing on Earth. It profits from your learning as you benefit from its learning. It loves to infuse your bodies with love and light, and to help you spiritualize matter and raise the frequency of your bodies and the energies around you that you naturally affect. There is also nothing to fear because, after all, your Higher Self is part of you. On the contrary, the "re-membering" of your Being is a true healing into wholeness.

6
Light Anchoring

St. Francis:

Light anchoring is one of the many functions of lightworkers. Of course, in the greater picture, everybody constantly anchors light or energy. We will use the two words "light" and "energy" interchangeably to get you used to the idea that light is energy and vice versa, even if frequencies might differ. In other words, on Earth you now live in slowed-down light. It is a denser form of light but no more or less divine and worthy.

We are also not just talking about people. This anchoring is done by animals, plants, trees, even rocks. All kingdoms are involved.

However, even while everybody is anchoring light or energy, some energies have specialized in this work. This means a lot of their energy is taken up with that task. Brian, of course, was one of those and many who have studied with him (if they are aware of their studies or not) are involved in anchoring what he has termed the Mahatma energy. Mahatma, Source, God, part of Source—we are not invested in names.

Light anchors use their bodies to "bring down the light." In other words, they open themselves up to be a vessel and have the energy stream through.

If you work as a light anchor, your Higher Self and your guides will monitor the energy input so that you do not "burn up." We do not want to scare anybody, but rather give you a sense of the power of this energy. If you have chosen—usually before you came into this body—to work in this way, be assured that you have guides working very closely with you, supporting this process.

Still, even though you trust and love your guides (you know them well from other lives and/or other dimensions), there are times where you might feel just too overwhelmed. Our channel has at times, told us to "lay off," especially when she feels too hot. We respect her wishes and do so, even when we can see that her system can handle more, with the appropriate rest, of course.

On the other hand, there was a time where she requested more energy. Although we saw that it was a bit too much, we followed her wishes so she could have the experience. She consequently got sick and learned about overtaxing the body. It was a good experience for her and she learned that more was not necessarily better.

There is a fine line between energy input, rest, sleep, movement, food input, fresh air, mental work, emotional work, stimulation from inside and outside, and other factors having to do with your other alternate realities. This is one reason why it is so important to follow your *own* Higher Self. Others do not know what your point of balance is. They might tell you to eat less or more, exercise less or more, work less or more. In short; they do not know. You need to turn to your own Self for such information.

Of course, you can seek support, love, friendship and general information if you desire. Then turn to your own Self and Source connection for verification. Only you know ultimately what is good for you.

Remember also that your body is changing. Some of the information described in medical text books does not apply to you anymore. Things are changing. Your bodies are changing. As a general rule, energy healing and more subtle forms of healing such as flower essences or homeopathic remedies are now preferable to remedy discomfort and illness. However, there are no "shoulds" here. If antibiotics work for you, then use them. *You need to decide for yourself by going inward.*

Now, here you are, at a certain point in your life, and suddenly the energy experiences start—heat, shaking, aches, undefinable pains, feelings of happiness and bliss—and a couple of days later a feeling of let down or "back to normal." Let us first of all say that everybody is very different and will experience this infusion of light and the integration of it very differently. Yes, there will be common themes and talking to your friends can be helpful, but there will also be differences. So know that you are on your individual path and that it is perfect. Our channel will share some of her experiences. Some of these you will experience as well and other elements you will probably never experience.

How much energy you channel or anchor depends on many factors. Let us cite a few of them: commitment, coding, and availability.

Commitment. How committed are you to this work? Are you willing to put up with inconvenience and even some ridicule? Are you willing to stick it out even though your personality is screaming at you, telling you to rejoin the so-called "real" world? We are joking to a certain extent, but the truth is that many more people could play a more active part in this ascension process if it were not so frightening to them to feel like "an odd ball out."

We do not judge, but we do wish that more people on Earth would remember the agreements that they made on higher levels. We know it is hard to stand out and we ask no-one to be very public unless that is what the soul chooses, but please join our efforts. Earth and all of the Beings in this universe would be helped in their evolution.

Please ask for a dream to show you how important your contribution here is. This contribution can be quiet, private, or it can be open and public. It does not matter but your participation is very, very important. Please do not let those energies that we call "con-fused" (fused with) convince you that you are insignificant. *That is a lie. Nobody is insignificant.*

Coding. You are coded for the work that you agreed to do on this planet, in this and other lifetimes. You see, you come from a family, a consciousness family, and certain purposes are coded in your DNA. Your purpose might be related to healing, communication, scientific endeavors, or providing certain structures. That does not mean that you will spend every lifetime with exactly that purpose but it will be in the back of your mind. Let us say that your spiritual family is very involved in healing and this lifetime you are a musician. Chances are that, in this life, in the back of your mind there is a recognition of the healing properties of music and in other realities, and in your dreams you are experimenting with this.

We suggest that you get a feel for your coding. What are you coded for? What is your purpose?

Availability. If you are a single parent with four children and two jobs trying to make ends meet, chances are that most of your "lightwork" will happen at night.

People are often surprised when they find out how practical we can be. Well, for one thing, many aspects of us have lived on Earth and many currently do, some in human form, but some of our energy is also in animals, the land, trees and plants. Please do not limit us to the pictures you see in Assisi.

Secondly, ascension is a very practical undertaking. We (meaning all of us involved in this project) are raising frequency to clean, clear, and let go of the fear-energies that have con-fused people, animals, plants and Earth for such a long time. In fact we (that is all of us, including you, dear reader) will try to transmute as much fear-energy as we can. Quite a clean up job, isn't it?

One more comment on availability: Sometimes your soul will make you available even if your personality is fighting it. Illness, job loss, divorce, or any other crisis can be created by your Higher Self. This has nothing to do with punishment or with God wanting you to suffer. You see, your personality might think your growth lies on a certain path whereas your soul knows that your true path might lie, for example, in anchoring light and increasing frequency. Again, it is for your optimum growth.

Call on your guides to help you through any hard times. They will be happy to hear you call. Do not feel you cannot bother them. *This is part of their "job description."* And they love you and get great joy from supporting you.

Anina on Light Anchoring and Integration:

First, I would like to share that I am becoming more and more aware how people's paths and purposes vary. In the end, we all have a common focus of enlightenment, optimal growth and awareness of our divinity but ways, goals, and interests differ.

I have found this to be also true among lightworkers, where there is a wide variety of interests and focuses. Some lightworkers are more interested in the scientific aspects of the process, such as earth grids, sacred geometry, or special healing techniques. Some are more interested in what I would call the philosophical aspects and how it fits all together, while others are very good at starting networks and facilitating the meeting of different energies. Some seem to need more stimulation, others find they need more quiet. Some lightworkers share their energies by traveling the world while others focus on one particular place.

I believe that many lightworkers do special work for the Earth, such as drawing out lower, denser energies that are no longer needed by the Earth. The lightworker transforms these with the help of his or her guides and friends. Furthermore, the person also brings in high frequency energies and anchors these into Earth. We all do this to some extent, but some people have specialized on this part of the "Ascension Project" and spend more time and effort doing this. They are often people who do not have many other responsibilities and love nothing more than being out in nature.

I cannot separate the process of light anchoring from the rest of my life (or should I say lives and alternate realities and dimensions). My work is also very connected with where I live, the other people around me who do this kind of work, my dog, the tree in front of my house, the Bach concerto on the radio—in short, *all is connected* and we all have a piece of the puzzle.

The first word that comes to mind when I hear the phrase "light anchoring" is resting. When Amy and I were channeling for each other, the most common words used by our guides were "relax, don't worry, rest your body, accept yourself, relax, don't worry, rest."

I find that people often underestimate the amount of energy needed to do this work. One factor in this ascension process is that as the energy pours through you, your body literally changes. During rest and sleep, our "electrical system" gets "rewired," our cells vibrate at a faster rate (some people react to this by getting dizzy and shaky), and our organs are being changed. (By the way, this has nothing to do with alien abductions or similar concepts. These are *your* Higher Self, *your* Being and *your* guides helping you to fulfill your purpose.)

Whenever my guides work with me I feel a sense of peace and trust, and I notice how my body relaxes. Sometimes there is some pain. One time, I had the feeling that I was going to get an ear infection and that they were they were poking around in my ear, trying to get the virus out. It hurt, and I said, "St. Francis, stop this."

"Sorry," I heard, "but we are trying to get the virus out."

At other times when I am just too exhausted to get worked on, I tell them to stop and they do so immediately.

It is interesting that guides often work on similar issues (be they physical, emotional, mental, or spiritual) on
different people at the same time. I like to connect with
my lightworker friends and exchange "work-in-progress"
reports. We are still astounded how often all our guides
are doing similar things. During one week, for example,
"working behind the eyeballs" was in fashion, and all four
of us had blurry vision. At other times, certain emotional
issues seem to be up for all of us at the same time, such as
anger at disempowerment, or sadness and grief.

My friend Martha once asked St. Francis why the
guides worked like that and he responded that it was more
powerful. He added that they, as guides, worked with
affirmations such as "you have perfect vision" and that it
was more powerful to link and work like that around the
globe.

I realize I sound pretty calm about all this. At times I
am and at other times—well, my phone company has a
record of those times. One of my friends once called and
after the usual "Hello," said, "Tell me I'm not crazy."

"You're not crazy," I responded. A couple of weeks
later I needed that same reassurance. I imagine that, years
from now, there will be talk shows about "ascension symptoms" by the so-called "experts." (I do not like the word
"expert" because I believe we all need to be our *own* au-
thority in this process.)

My process is a continuing exploration in which I am
reminded to *accept myself at all times* and to go step-by-
step, moment-by-moment, with trust and faith that I am
part of a wonderful project. I have been very lucky to have
had many dreams, experiences and help from many energies—with and without physical bodies. I feel that I am
part of this wonderful puzzle/project and I have to do my
piece—not more, not less, just my piece.

Clearing Fear

In this context, let me talk about fear. Here is how it works from what I have learned and experienced so far. First, you take in light, either by participating in a workshop, praying, or simply lying on the couch feeling your guides working on you. I experience taking in light mainly as heat in my body. It is very pleasurable, but sometimes my wrists ache afterwards or something else that was worked on hurts. Emotionally, I usually feel the love and peace from my guides and I feel virtually lighter and more peaceful.

Then, often a couple of days later, "stuff" comes up. Sometimes I get frustrated and exclaim, "I thought I had already dealt with this. Why is this coming up again?" Part of me knows it is coming from a deeper level and a more profound healing is taking place, but in the moment, I am often aggravated. "I am sick of clearing," I can hear myself say. Or, "I thought I had it all together."

Remember the light infusion itself was wonderful. I felt connected, on the right path, sure that my guides love me, and so on. What has happened is that the greater light in my body has brought up denser energies that are now ready to be released.

Sometimes when I am in fear, it feels like being in a cloud. I keep forgetting that clearing follows light infusion. Of course, fear can do that to us. When we can love ourselves in the midst of that fear and judgment, we can move through it as lovingly and mercifully as possible in each moment.

Pace

Everybody will have her or his own pace in this process. Pace depends on many elements. St. Francis mentioned some of them—your plans before incarnating (and plans can change), your availability, other responsibilities and aspects of your purpose, the ease with which you can move through this process and how much work you agree to have done on yourself by your Self. As all bodies (spiritual, mental, emotional and physical) are affected, all of them need to move on together. In my case, and the same has been true for many of my friends, the body that seems to lag behind most often is the physical body.

There are many reasons for this. One is that this ascension process is, in many ways, a very physical process. After all, what we are doing is bringing light into every cell of the body or, if you prefer, reminding the body of who it is ultimately—slowed down light.

There are many ways to support the body in this process: communing with nature, energy healing, polarity work, flower essences, herbs, massage, movement, color and sound therapy, and other modalities. As we progress in this mass ascension experience, pioneers will come up with new tools such as new forms of healing, new flower essences and other inventions. However, in my opinion, rest will always be part of the equation. The transition to higher frequencies will become easier and better understood, but it is still quite a bit of work for a body to raise its vibration.

At one point I asked my guides to speed up the process. For a week, one lesson came after another, and I experienced constant beeping and heat sensations every night. I was being worked on every second of the day.

"All right, all right," I said after the week was up. "I get it. New affirmation: I grow with joy and ease."

I heard them laughing, "So you want more fun in your life."

Well, that was another experience in free will. My guides often give me exactly what I want or think I want so that I can explore to see if I *really* want it.

The right pace in the ascension process is still a mystery to me. Often, less is more. Remember, after these fantastic healings and frequency highs, the new energy has to be integrated into the four bodies. What people are able to take in is very individual, and of course your Higher Self knows what is best for you.

At one point I listened to Brian's meditation tapes for one hour each day. His tapes transmit vibrations of a very high frequency. So there I was, week after week, continually bathing in light and spiritual concepts. One day I awoke and could not move. I finally made it out of bed and talked to my body. I was upset.

"What do you want?" I asked belligerently. "I slowed down my life, I moved to the country, I exercise, I meditate…"

"Relaxation," I heard.

"But," I protested, "I meditate and I do Brian's tapes…"

"That is not relaxation," I heard back.

Then I got it. All this bathing in light and golden white Mahatma energy was not relaxing for the body. After all it was light infusion, and, as wonderful as this light infusion is, it needs to be integrated.

These days, I listen to Brian's tapes when I am guided to. During times of light integration, I often listen to very basic relaxation tapes where I go through my body and release any tension that I feel.

Exercise and Movement

Again, we need to listen to ourselves. Your Higher Self knows exactly how much exercise and movement you need. When Amy and I began channeling for each other, our guides continued to tell us to rest and slow down. One day Amy shook her head and exclaimed, "I do not know how we can slow down even more."

Amy and I call those days our "couch days"—"resting" being one of our main occupations. In those days, I was guided to exercise very slowly. Later this changed, and I started to buy some faster music.

Nowadays I often need to move after a channeling, and especially after readings, I need to ground the energy by moving my legs. One exercise I enjoy is moving my feet while standing. At some point, my legs start shaking and I can feel the energy moving down into the ground. I love to just follow my body and experiment.

Our guides told Amy and me that the amount of movement, activity, or rest needed is individual for everybody. It depends, among other factors, on a person's blueprint and what type of energy they are. I once gave a reading to a friend where St. Francis told her that a good image for her was one of a black horse. She has a lot of power and needs a fair amount of movement. "Our channel," he added, "is more like a turtle. Everybody is different."

I was not pleased. "A turtle," I said to her later, "does not sound very exciting to me."

"But, Anina" she said in her sweet way, "don't you know that, according to native teachings, the turtle carries the Earth on her back?"

"Okay, then" I sighed, "turtle it is."

7

Working with Emotions

St. Francis:

Likes and Dislikes and Rules

It is natural for a personality to have likes and dislikes. That is part of how a person maneuvers in this world. Now, there are those who say it is "unspiritual" to like and dislike. There are those who might tell you that you need to love everybody and be grateful for any situation in your life. This is not true and not practical in the world of duality. This is a hard one for many because years of so-called religious training have taught you "the rules." Well, in the bigger picture, there are no rules.

There are laws, yes, but they are much more impersonal, such as the law of gravity as it applies on Earth, or the law of giving and receiving. However, rules? There are none.

This does not mean there is no discipline or responsibility. But it is *natural* discipline. Let us give you an example. A flower stretches its head towards the sun, not because somebody told it to do so but because it gives the flower joy. It is natural and "respons-able" to receive the sun and its love and warmth.

When you get up in the morning, it is natural to stretch and move your body. You do not need an exercise expert to tell you how to move your body. All you need to do is listen. Listen to your body, your inner self, your love inside of you. If it gives you joy to move to music with others in what is called a fitness class then, by all means do so. If you hate that, then you might consider a different method, because joy is important in your lives. More and more, joy will become the driving force. Follow your heart, your creativity, and whatever makes your soul sing.

Emotions

Along with having been told not to dislike certain people or situations, many of you have been told that anger is bad. Anger is *not* bad. Let us repeat: There is nothing evil about anger.

Violence is a different matter. In fact, violence arises when anger and other emotions have not been appropriately expressed, as in a pressure cooker where steam continues to collect until the top flies off. Those of you with the habit of collecting steam need to learn to open the valve slowly and to "let off steam" carefully.

Some of you blow off loudly for everyone to see. Others do it silently, and many attack their bodies by quietly turning unresolved emotions inward. The body lovingly holds emotions for you; it is a friend.

We do not have a judgment on any form of emotional release. We know that, at times, life in the physical can be very difficult. We do not judge. We just observe and give you feedback if you wish to look at those patterns with us.

Expressing Emotions

We will focus on anger because, for many of you, that is the hardest one to look at. Some of you find it easy to cry but hard to allow the word "no" to emerge. For some, it is the other way round.

Emotions are energy in motion. Ultimately, you and I and this whole universe are energy—love/energy we like to call it. If you experience an emotion, that means you (an energy gestalt yourself) feel energy flowing through you. In fact that is very much how we experience e-motion. We actually experience it as an energy gestalt that we interact with. Since we do not have judgment as you do, we do not have a problem with it. For us, it is just energy.

Question by Anina: "How is your judgment different from the judgment we have?"

Okay. Let us answer this first. We have judgment without fear, which some of us here have termed "discernment." It is hard for you in the physical to understand judgment without fear because fear is so pervasive on this planet. It is a bit like choosing from a dinner menu. You say, for example, "No, I do not want the rice dish tonight. I want lasagna instead." This does not mean that you are afraid of rice, or that you chose lasagna out of fear. You are just discerning, deciding what you would prefer. We hope this gives you the idea. It is hard to grasp the concept of non-judgment in the physical.

Since emotions are just energy, we often ask you to give up your emotions to your guides. They love to take them and transform them, but they need your permission because you have free will. In order to give up those emotions, you have to take them out of your closets. Anger that is stuck in your liver is hard for us to get at, although we try.

Also, please do not judge yourselves for hiding your emotions. Many grew up in environments that taught, "Do not get angry, do not cry." Add to this all your lives as monks and nuns trying to be "better than the Pope" and you can see that it is not easy to be an authentic human being.

So if your closet is very full, then you need to open it slowly or chances are you will feel overwhelmed. Take out those energy clutters a little at a time, and know that it gets easier as time goes along. Follow your Higher Self's timing. It is your greater Self that knows when to proceed more quickly and when you need to go very, very slowly.

Cleaning Out The Closets

We would like to offer you a visualization that might be helpful. Read this to yourself, or let a friend or therapist read it, or put it on tape. See your process either as an internal movie, or create your own pictures, or write it as a story starting with, for example, "Today, I decided to clean my closets."

Get comfortable, whether sitting or lying down, and feel your Higher Self and guides with you. You might see them, hear them or feel a presence. You might just visualize an angel, for all of you have a guardian angel regardless of whether you can see him or her. Call on us if that feels right. Whether you can sense us or not, we are present when called upon.

See yourself in a beautiful house. Visualize its rooms and notice that, although they are beautiful, there is a bit too much clutter. You decide to clean up, slowly, and in your own time. Nobody is pushing you. You are in control. You are the creator of your destiny and you have unlimited support. Your Higher Self, your angels, and many other old friends are standing by. Ascended masters are available to help you. There is nothing to worry about. In fact, this can be fun.

You slowly open the door of one of the closets and see all kinds of things in there. A lot of what you see are little toy cubes in different colors. The red ones represent anger and other colors represent other energy clusters. You want to take out all of them, but decide to take only one. You pick a red one and then close the door. You notice how calm you are and give the cube to one of your guides. Your guide takes the cube and transforms it into a beautiful light. Its energy is free now and ready to create on a higher level. It is likely to come back to you and help you to lighten up your life and body.

You are astounded how easy all this was. Now slowly come back to here and now.

After you have completed the exercise, please let it go. Go for a walk or find some other activity. Please do not think any more about this exercise. Things are in motion and the best you can do now is to leave it alone and clear the way. The mind tends to try and create a problem, "Did I do it right? Am I going to become a better person from doing such an exercise?" *Let it go.*

In the course of reading this book, you might notice dreams where the material brought up by this exercise is being processed and "played with." We prefer to call it "played with" rather than worked with, because we would like to introduce you to the idea that this process of ascension and "lightening up" can be fun. It is not always comfortable, but even that does not need to keep you from having fun.

Know that your greater Self never gives you more than you can handle. Know also that you can say "no" to your guides. Your guides love you unconditionally, which means there are no conditions to their love. You do not need to earn it. In fact, you cannot make your guides (or God for that matter) *not* love you. It is impossible.

Let us come back to dreams for a moment. We suggest that you take notice of your dreams, especially the ones with houses, closets, (power) animals, religious symbols, and interactions with others. If you have suppressed the energy of anger, you might have dreams where you say "no" to people.

If vulnerability has been your great fear, you might be asked to trust or you might recognize the vulnerable part of yourself in one of your dream figures—a person, a little bird or another trusting creature, for example. You might also get in touch with another past/parallel life where you were able to trust. This life might be reaching out to you to help you find balance. So have fun. This process can be exciting and invigorating.

Emotions In The Body

E-motions (and we spell the word this way to remind you that these are just energy in motion) often get stored in your bodies.

You have an emotional, a spiritual, a mental, and a physical body. All of these bodies have the same original blueprint, what we call your light body. On a higher dimension, these bodies are pure light.

Part of the ascension process is raising the frequency of all your bodies to align with your lightbody. At some point you will actually look lighter, and sometimes people will notice a translucent quality to your vehicle. What you are doing is bringing down the light and spiritualizing matter.

In a way, the term "spiritualizing matter" is not correct, because matter is spirit too. As all that exists is part of All That Is or Source, so bodies and rocks are also part of God. However we feel the visual picture of "spiritualizing matter" can be helpful in the process. Some people talk about descension and use the concept of spirit coming down and infusing the vehicle. Others prefer the idea of ascension. It does not matter, both are correct. Please, as always, use what feels right to you.

As your four bodies raise their vibration, emotions and any other form of lower density energy gets released. We have given our channel the picture of a centrifugal machine where the heavier material gets thrown or spun out. It is very similar to the process you all go through.

Some of you will find the process easier than others. It depends on your original blueprint, crystalline structure, relationship with your bodies, "past lives," belief structure and, most of all, on your capacity to accept yourself or to allow your greater Self's love to come through and comfort you. Let us explain, step by step.

Original Blueprint

All of you are part of All That Is, part of Source. All of you have an original blueprint or energy structure.

Let us use the analogy of a puzzle. If the big puzzle represents All That Is, then you and we would represent pieces of the puzzle. In truth, our energy gestalt is not any bigger than yours, but in your framework, we are bigger because we are more connected. While some of you still feel alone and isolated, we have realized that we are part of a whole and have actually connected with some of our appropriate puzzle pieces—without losing our individual "puzzle-pieceness."

Now, please visualize the puzzle expanding. All That Is, as well as its individual conscious and unconscious parts, are constantly expanding. There is nothing static in this or other universes. This explains why even something as apparently solid as an energetic blueprint is actually subject to change. On a bodily level, the DNA, which is a physical blueprint and seemingly unalterable, is also subject to change.

Again, nothing is static in this universe. All is moving. If this frightens you, dear reader, please remember that *all* change is propelled by love and all these universes are permeated by the love of God (or Source) for all of its creation. Change is only frightening if you resist it. If you let yourself be carried by it, it can be as pleasant as a soft breeze stroking you on a warm summer day.

The movement itself is *Love*. If you could tune deeply into your body, there is a chance you could actually hear it humming, hear the electrons spinning. This is a tone of joy, dear ones, and a body that is allowed to relax and be delights in its own movement and change.

Now, let us give you examples of blueprints. We have often, with our channel, used the analogy of an orchestra to help her understand different energies. We have described our energy as that of a cello—deep, strong, peaceful and calming. Since she is part of our soul group or greater Self, her true energy is the same. Channeling us is very healing for her because she gets in touch with who she really is, with her own energy. She, like some of you, at times gets "con-fused" with other energies. So it is vital for her to get back to her own true note.

There are some of you who are like triangles—very refined, very soft and delicate and often very attuned to the stars. You want to sparkle, and at the same time you need your space. You want to add your gentle healing tone but do not like to get stuck between a trumpet and a clarinet. Some of you have found it very hard to be on Earth and live in this density. At night you often whiz around among the stars. Those of you who had a lot of work to complete in the third-dimensional world often needed heavy armor to get through it all. Often people experienced you as distant or not accessible—because you were. You had to be to survive. Some of you are very excited about the new times because you feel that it is time to give up some of that heavy armor. It has served you well.

Oh, and then there are the trumpets, the ones who go out and toot their own horn. They are often the bold ones. They are the ones who do not care about the details but know how to get started. Trumpets are great ones to help you get moving, to make that first step and get started. Trumpets usually do not have a problem with change and at times get impatient at those "doodlers," as they sometimes perceive others, such as the triangle who is waiting for the exact timing to share its exquisite note. Trumpets usually do not have a hard time with other energies and seldom feel overwhelmed. They love to move and give their bodies lots of exercise. They do benefit, however, from the quieter ones, and can learn to appreciate the beauty of silence, the notes between the notes as we like to call it.

Our channel has friends who are attuned to Jesus' energy. His core energy is one of love and sweetness. He also adds an expansiveness to other energies and helps entities to grow and open their hearts. All of us here can, of course, provide any energy that we want to channel to you, but you will usually also experience our base energy.

Our channel has likened Jesus' energy to the sound of a violin sweetly singing her song. There is some truth to that. Another entity we know has likened her energy to sparkles in the sky or light dancing on water.

It is important now for all of you to explore and play with the idea of energy. What does *your* energy feel like when you feel good? What pictures, images, and associations come to mind when you feel centered? Is there deep peace, excitement, the flight of the eagle, or the joy of fireworks?

Crystalline Structure

Your crystalline structure has more to do with your actual body. What is it like? How are you built? What energies and genes have you taken on from your parents, your ancestors, even your country to an extent? Many of those incarnating in formerly war-torn countries are still affected by the fear energies that were caught in their grandparents' bodies at the time of a bombing, for example.

By the way, you would each know all about that before coming. You each *decide* to take on certain energies so as *to help clear and transmute* them. This is *not* about victimhood. Now, that does not mean that you will always like it, or even understand it on a personality level, and that is all right. The clearing happens because you, as the powerful creator you are, decided it will happen.

Your current crystalline structure is very connected to the crystalline structures of so-called past lives. Of course, they are not really past; they are happening literally right *now*. In fact, as you move more and more into your "relative now" (the now that you can experience on Earth), your "past lives" are coming closer. Your life becomes more multi-dimensional and you might have various dreams, flashes, or experiences of past lives and alternate realities (these are paths not taken but considered as probable at one time, and played out in other realities).

As you heal this body, your "parallel bodies" are being healed as well, and you begin to integrate your various cells and experiences. Again, there is nothing you have to do. It will all occur quite naturally and your Higher Self will guide you. *Trust yourself.*

This leads us to your belief structure. How much do you believe in yourself? How much have you been taught to believe in outer authorities? In short, how much do you love yourself and trust your inner voice and wisdom? We will talk more about this throughout the book.

Anina On Emotional And Physical Clearing:

I find St. Francis' observations on clearing—not only for ourselves, but also for our ancestors, nation, and possibly humanity itself—very interesting. The whole area is still quite a mystery to me but I am becoming more and more aware of how we are all connected and how what we do for our Self we also do for others. If we clear certain patterns, then we open the door for others as well. They will be able to release these patterns much more quickly and easily if we have already done so. It seems to me that nobody is an island and everybody is connected.

During Brian's last seminar in Basel, he suggested to us that if we ever felt lonely or frustrated we could call on the energies of the group. We had created a powerful group vehicle and I sometimes do call on these energies when I need support. I believe we all have such groups. There is a whole network of friends out there, some in body and some not embodied, some we have met and some we have not met yet or will not meet in this lifetime. In my dreams I sometimes work with other lightworkers, some whom my present personality knows and some whom "Anina" does not know, but that "I," the greater I, knows.

8

More on Emotions

St. Francis:

Accept yourself, accept yourself, accept yourself. From where we are, we can see all the fear and heaviness you all carry around very clearly. *This is not you.*

Yes, this is energy, just as you are energy, but on another level *it is not you.* You are not "your" fear, "your" depression, "your" sadness; just like the tea in our channel's cup is not the cup. The cup is the container, the tea is a "friend" hanging out there for a while. For many it is helpful to remember this because in fear, many feel con-fused. What you do is literally fuse your energy with the energy of fear, which was either picked up from another person, directly or via cable [amused], or was just floating around as a thoughtform.

Some say, "Like attracts like." In other words, if you do not have any fear, you will not "attract" any. We feel that this statement has a grain of truth, but that it is also somewhat simplistic. Remember, if you live on Earth you will have a personality and will experience emotions. Or, to use an analogy, if you are in the middle of the ocean you will get wet, no matter how many people tell you that a "truly evolved being" should be able to stay dry. We are, of course, joking.

So here you are, living on Earth, in the midst of all this energy in motion. Our channel is asking how this all fits with the idea of creating your own reality. Well, on one level of your Being (and we do not even like to call it higher, but let us say one that has a more expansive point of view), you have agreed to come to Earth knowing full well that it means experiencing emotions such as love, joy, anger, sadness, and others. Again, you are not a victim. You agreed to this.

Many of you have come particularly to help clear up some of these emotions. Our channel used to sit with people who had a lot of fear. She willingly took on some of their fear to help them lighten their load. This does not mean that our channel did not learn her own lessons in this work, or that she herself had no fear. But there was an agreement that she had made before incarnating that her personality was not aware of. When the agreement was fulfilled, she lost interest in this kind of work and moved on. As she became more consciously involved in her ascension process, she needed to let go of fear (within and without) to become "lighter." So you see, there is purpose, timing and there are no rules.

For many of you now, the *clearing* is one of the hardest parts of this ascension process. Again, there are no rules, and everybody is different. Some will need to clear more anger, others will clear more sadness or physical discomfort. It is all connected with your purpose, your many lives and realities, and your ability to stay focused and connected to your Higher Self. The more you can detach from the process and not judge, the easier it will be.

We know it sounds so simple, and that is why some of you find it so difficult. You have been taught that the process is difficult, not just in your schools of psychology and philosophy but also in the so-called mystery schools of the past: Egypt and Atlantis, for instance.

"Ascension is a secret." "Only the purest are worthy." "Initiations are secret." "This is not for the masses, the unworthy." Is any of this ringing a bell? So here are we, St. Francis, talking about *mass ascension* and we would like to add that it can be easy and simple, especially if you go moment to moment and follow your own truth and guidance.

So emotions are not a problem. Emotions are emotions. The more you can detach and love yourself in the process of experiencing the e-motion moving through you, the easier it can be.

Many of you have been told that it is "bad" to be angry or sad. *That is a lie.* It is as simple as that. It is *not bad* to be sad. It just is. It is not good either. Some have tried to turn their conditioning around by reversing some of the beliefs. This might work for a while but, ultimately, emotion is just energy in motion.

Two words that we like to use in describing the process of clearing are "expressing" and "recycling." Expressing emotions is part of clearing. Recycling emotions is *not* clearing. It is more of a "mind-activity" and is used by the ego as a defense against expression. Some people describe this process as "rehashing the old" or going over an issue that is long gone and past, over and over again. "Recycling" is certainly not about being in the present moment. Often people who have active minds use this strategy to defend against real emotions located in the physical body or any other bodies.

Again, there is no perfect way to clear, and everybody's experience and challenges will vary, but "recycling" is one activity that makes it harder and often more painful to clear. You see, in truth it is not the personality that is "in charge of clearing." It is your Self that knows exactly what you need and what is right for you from moment to moment. Clearing is most effortless when you can keep the ego out and let yourself just be who you are.

Let us get very practical. Typical ego responses are, "I should not be tired. I should not be sad. Let me try to cry so that I can get over this depression," and so on. You have heard it all.

So, let us assume you are sad and you let yourself be that way. You do not need to focus on it or even interrupt your activity (maybe you are just washing the dishes or folding laundry). All you need to do is: *Notice it and do not judge yourself.* Maybe you get angry at yourself for being sad. *Notice that.* Maybe you start eating to drown the feeling. *Notice that and love yourself* in the midst of judgment. Call on your Higher Self and your guides to help you *be with yourself.* Know that deep down you know how to be with yourself without criticism. Do not try to do it "perfectly;" just go step by step, moment to moment. Your Higher Self might guide you to sit down to rest or meditate or write or to just continue with the dishes or whatever you were doing. *Listen to yourself.*

Suppose you are now in a more loving state. Usually the energy (of the e-motion) will now simply move through you, or maybe it will not. Accept that as well. Many of you will now get insights, but many of you will not. Remember, clearing is not just personal. You are also clearing for others and for your other lives. Chances are, the longer you are on the ascension path the less information you will get about particular feelings moving through. And *you do not need the information.* Your Higher Self knows and leads the way.

We are giving our channel the picture of a cab driver. Your Higher Self is the cab driver and knows where you are going. Your anxiety about where you are going, and your con-fused suggestions to the cab driver, are not really helping. (And your ego will probably hate this analogy.)

We are not talking about surrendering to another, following another entity. No, we are talking about the foot and the head moving in harmony. We are talking about trusting your Self.

Anina:

I would like to share some of my process and specifically my struggle with accepting anger.

I used to firmly believe that anger was unspiritual. I used to believe that the goal in life was to become a "good person," and that once one was good enough, one was granted some kind of spiritual bonus. This kind of thinking was supported in this life by a cultural system where saying "no" was "unlady-like" or simply too scary. In addition, I believe I had several monk lives and have carried over many rigid and self-denying "spiritual" beliefs from these lives.

Imagine my surprise when my guides encouraged me to feel my anger and be with it. "Yes, but ..." was my usual answer. At times I would wake up in the middle of the night in rages, and I had a whole series of dreams in which I said "no" to people that I felt unable to stand up to in "real" life. One friend who used to try to "therapize" me came in a dream and I turned toward her and said in a firm voice, "Don't tell me what to do!"

St. Francis and Amy's guides applauded my dreamwork. I myself was not so sure. But my feeling of well-being improved and people kept telling me that I looked healthier and stronger.

My guides have many times stated that they do not have a judgment on emotion. "For us, it is just energy," they used to say. They encouraged me to accept sadness, anger, frustration, depression, or whatever else, and to just let it go through me. They encouraged me to give it to them because they could transform the energy.

Obviously to "just be with it" and "accept it" is often easier said than done. "Easy for you to say," I would grumble back at times. My anger and frustration were always received with unconditional love, and at times with love and some amusement.

I have found that for me, music and dance or other movement is very helpful. If angry, I would put on some energetic music, if sad, there was always the Blues.

I would like to share one more experience I had with releasing anger. I believe it shows how we can truly give up a lot of the "work" to our Higher Self and our dream self.

One day I suddenly felt all kinds of anger about somebody that I had not seen or even talked to for a long time. It was old anger that came up after another light infusion.

Maybe it had been hiding out in one of my organs. Anyway, as St. Francis often tells me, I do not need to know all the details.

My guides told me to write a letter, not to be sent, but to express my anger and rage. I did and I felt I had made some good points. I thought about sharing it with a friend but St. Francis suggested not to do that, and to burn the letter instead. He told me it was important to express and let go, express and let go. He added that with this letter, I had started a process and needed to keep it fresh and clean. "There is no need to look back," he concluded. "Stay in the moment."

I soon forgot about the letter and had two subsequent dreams with the person that I had been angry at. I forgot the first dream but in the second one he came into a room while I was sleeping and verbally insulted me.

I got up and yelled, "I need to be respected! You need to respect all people regardless of profession or education or any such things. All people need to be respected." I added, "You do not need to accept everybody and like them, but you have to respect them." Then I woke up.

For me, this experience was one of many lessons in letting my Higher Self resolve an issue.

9

Subpersonalities and "Decision-Making"

Anina:

I believe that we have many facets to our personality. To make this more complex, we are also influenced by our past/parallel lives and alternate realities. And ultimately, we are all energy. In fact, our guides told Amy and myself many times that this is how they see us— as energy.

As an energy field, we each have all kinds of frequencies going on. As we raise our main frequency, lower density energy is being raised or let go of, and transmitted into the light.

Within this framework, our subpersonalities are energy too. St. Francis once showed me a circle and cut it almost into halves. He told me that I had split myself into halves, the "good" part and the supposedly "bad" part. By not accepting certain parts of myself and putting them into a closet, so to speak, I had literally split them off.

"We cannot ascend what you hacked in half," St. Francis said. I realized that if I wanted to raise my frequency, I first had to become whole and accept all parts of myself.

Through readings, I met several people who have accepted their assertive parts but have judged against their "weak part," the "vulnerable part," the "whiny part." I have found the work is always similar: Accept, accept, accept. Bring it to the light and love that part of yourself.

In my work with my guides, the first step in working with my subpersonalities was safety. I came to a point where I felt safe with my guides and was able to allow more love in. Then St. Francis asked me to allow in those parts of myself that I was judging. A lot of the work happened in dreams, where I created all kinds of dramas and gave my subpersonalities interesting roles. The "lazy part," for example, stood up to a workaholic boss. The "mean part" told off an old friend. In one dream I said to her, "Don't tell me what to do and how to be."

At some point St. Francis seemed to feel the time was right for a more direct encounter. He asked me to get some paper and to start writing with the sentence: "I am bad and deserve to be punished because ..."

Well, I wrote and wrote, and was genuinely surprised at the beliefs that came up. I started a dialog with parts of myself that I now call "my guys," and with the help of my greater Self, we talked. "My guys" told the personality (or the "nice" part I was conscious of) that she was often naive and let people walk all over her. They said, "We could have told you X was a power monger, but you would not listen to us. No, you have to smile all the time, have to pretend everything is wonderful, can't see clearly." I had to admit, they were right.

Slowly I developed a friendship with this part of me and with St. Francis' help, I made peace with "the guys." We did not trust each other in the beginning but appreciation for each other grew. I came to admire this part of my personality for its power of observation. "The guys" always cut right through certain ego games and could not be fooled.

The other work that Amy and I did around sub-personalities involved writing. I completed a novel where many parts of myself were allowed to speak. I received the first "scene" of this novel in a dream. Now I see clearly that the novel was just for me to enable myself to *express* parts of myself that I had suppressed.

At one point, my friend Amy was asked to write "whiny" letters to a friend who constantly "whined" to her. Amy has always despised "whining" and—surprise,

surprise—"whiny" people kept appearing in front of her. St. Francis suggested that she "free the whiner within" by writing letters that did not need to be sent but were meant as a vehicle of expression. We had a lot of fun with this. Since I can be an "expert whiner," I helped her.

"No," I said, after reading the first letter, "not whiny enough." After looking over the second letter, I told her that she was not very good at this and needed to try harder.

She got back at me when I wrote my angry letters. "You call that angry?" she said with a mischievous smile. "You better try again."

Coming back to the concept of energy, if we suppress parts of ourselves, then we are really suppressing energy. This means we lose energy by putting parts of ourselves into a "closet," and we lose additional energy by pressing against the door to keep it shut. I guess that sometimes suppressing parts of ourselves is the best we can do at a particular point in time, but eventually I believe we need to free ourselves, especially when we start raising our frequency.

In recent times I have talked to many who were asked to make major decisions, such as whether to leave a job, a relationship, or a physical location. When my friends asked St. Francis for help, his answer was often the same, "It is a process," he would say in his calm and comforting tone.

At times he gave me the picture of an apple ripening on a tree. He suggested to my friends to wait until the fruit was ready, then they could pick it easily and be sure it was a good decision.

He often told people that, on a Higher Self level, they had not yet made a decision and needed to be patient.

He reminded my friends and myself that we were part of a bigger plan and purpose. During times of indecision he asked us to focus on our purpose.

"What is your goal?" he once asked a friend in a reading.

"Ascension," she replied, and St. Francis nodded. She decided to focus on her writing, meditation, and living from moment-to-moment without yet knowing about the potential life choice.

St. Francis often reminds me that since we are all connected, one person's highest good is also for other people's highest good. (I am, of course, talking about highest good as seen by the Higher Self and not the ego.)

Sometimes our Higher Self is waiting to make a decision because it is impacted upon by the Higher Self decisions of others. For example, on a Higher Self level, one person might ask another to move to their area. Maybe there is the probability of a close relationship, or maybe part of one's spiritual family lives at this new location. Maybe this area needs another light anchor and this person's energy would harmonize well in this physical environment. Sometimes the land itself can call us.

As with all decisions in the world of duality, there are advantages and disadvantages. Maybe we are needed where we live at this moment. Maybe we are supporting people energetically and practically where we are right now. Maybe there are still some wonderful lessons to be learned exactly where we are now.

Even if we move and meet the people we were "supposed" to meet, there is another element: personalities and their free will. Let us say that we were planning, on a Higher Self level, for a wonderful relationship with somebody, a relationship with a great lesson plan for both of us. It is very possible that one of the personalities gets scared and says, "No, this is all too much of a stretch. I prefer the old familiar way." Well, lesson plans have to be changed and readjusted with the main goal always in mind. This goal I believe is, for all of us, ascension, enlightenment, or personal growth.

When our Higher Self leads us to major change, there are usually many factors involved. Often one of them is letting go of conditioning and dying to the old. This is not always comfortable, but I believe that if we trust our Higher Self, we will eventually see the wisdom of the decision of the soul.

How Subpersonalities Affect Decision-Making

At some point I realized that through connecting with all parts of myself, decision-making has become much easier. In fact, it feels almost as if I do not make any decisions anymore. I feel I watch them evolve naturally from a process of cooperation and communication.

I used to dread decisions for fear of making the "wrong one." Friends of mine would make fast and impulsive decisions out of discomfort with ambivalence. I believe each method is out of balance and does not produce our highest good. Now I often see a picture of a "round table" where my subpersonalities sit and express themselves. I see my Higher Self as a facilitator giving each energy, love, and acceptance. Many times I invite other Beings such as Archangel Gabriel, Jesus, and others.

My work is now focused on expressing all parts of myself. Let me give you an example. I recently pondered a physical move. As always in duality, there were advantages and disadvantages to moving. On the one hand I was yearning for the countryside, on the other I had many good friends in the city. There were, of course, more voices. There was the part of me that loves being alone. And, especially since I had become more aware of my sensitivity and more attuned to receiving energy and information from other people, part of me now wanted more space. Another part of me was afraid to be alone. Part of me loved the idea of the move and had a sense of adventure. Another part said, "Stay were you are. Do not change your life. It is all right now."

I listened to all parts and expressed them freely on paper, in dreams, and with friends. I did not try to value one more than another or suppress any part. In the past I might have told myself something like, "Get over your fear of loneliness. You need to be independent" (whatever that meant for me at the time).

At some point, things just started to happen. We found the perfect home and I connected with people at the new place. In general the whole move was effortless.

Expressing Versus Making Things Into Problems

In a reading, St. Francis suggested to a friend of mine to express different parts of herself that could help her to make a certain decision. He encouraged her to talk to friends "as long as," he added with a smile, "they do not make your process into a problem."

"Now I understand why I always hesitate to talk to others," she said to me after the reading. "They usually make things into a problem."

Again, I believe that the key is acceptance. If we can express a part of ourselves that seeks expression and then hold it in the light of acceptance, then we can literally raise the energy of this part of ourselves and re-integrate it into our Being. So-called negative thoughts and feelings can be brought to the light and transmuted to a higher frequency.

There is an old metaphysical law that says that if you focus on a problem you actually make it bigger. I personally used to believe that I had to focus intensely on a problem in order to solve it. It took me a long time to learn to relax and to look at problems in a more detached and relaxed way. Two things that helped me most with this were living more in the *now*, and dealing with one thing at a time without focusing on solving a problem. Instead I learned to *look* at it step by step and to *allow* a solution to come naturally. I believe a preconceived solution can keep us from letting in another solution, one that is for our highest good.

In readings, people often present a problem and ask, "What should I do?" Usually St. Francis will not focus on the question or the problem but explores with the person the underlying assumptions. Often the assumptions are beliefs such as, "I have to make compromises; I cannot get what I really want because I have to consider person X, who wants me to behave in a certain way; I need to make do with what I do not want; I do not deserve what would really give me joy."

It is very interesting how, when the framework is expanded and certain limiting beliefs are put aside for a moment, new options that were not even considered before arise. Often one of these options feels good and people choose that, or they go home and open up their framework some more to see what happens.

"In truth, there are no problems," our guides have often told us. "Easy for you to say," Amy and I have often countered, but at times we get a glimpse of the truth of the statement.

In readings with Amy's guide, I used to ask about certain decisions. "What should I do?" I would lament.

"You have a choice," she would reply, and in the beginning I disliked that response.

"But what is the right thing to do?" I would insist. "There is no 'right thing,'" she would counter. "There is choice A, B, or C and they all have advantages and disadvantages."

In hindsight I can see that a lot of my discomfort with the idea of choices came from a fear that if I did the "wrong thing" I would be punished. That was old conditioning, and once I was able to release a lot of these old beliefs, I began to enjoy the idea of choices and freedom.

Another false concept that would "haunt" me was the idea of "missing out." I would ask Amy's guide about a workshop and her response usually was, "You can go or you can not go."

"But what if I do not go and I miss out on something? What if this was *the* workshop or *the* teacher which could bring me enlightenment? What if I miss a great opportunity?" were some of my questions.

Again, in hindsight the beliefs underlying this kind of thinking were around someone or something outside myself "saving me." Now I see clearly that I do not need anyone or anything outside of myself, and furthermore, I do not really need to "save myself." I need to accept and *be* myself.

This is not to say that workshops and seminars cannot be fun, and that the joining of group energy is not a powerful tool for healing and transformation. But now I try to make sure I want to go to a seminar because I *want* to, and not because of an old belief that there is something terribly wrong with me and that I need to be "fixed."

Probable Futures And Highest Good

Nothing in our future is etched in stone. I believe that when genuine psychics tell us our future, they just tap into certain probabilities. I also believe that a psychic will focus on those probabilities that are closest to his or her vibration. If a psychic in his or her life focuses on doom and gloom, then he or she will, in my view, most likely pick up on our probabilities of doom and gloom. This does not mean the psychic is "wrong" as such; it is just another example of how the perceiver and the perceived are intimately connected.

I believe that what we need to do is to align ourselves from moment to moment with the highest probability possible.

10

Centering, Holding a Vision, and Discernment

Anina:

For me, the concepts of centering, holding a vision, and practicing discernment are all connected.

Before I start to envision, for example, a healthy body, a healthy planet, or peace in a war-torn country, I get centered. St. Francis often says that we create from our intention. If we come from a place of love, we will create more love. If we come from fear and guilt, we will eventually create more fear and guilt. At times, we act from a place that is less than clear, and while we think we are "helping" others and looking out for everybody's best interest, we are, in reality, coming from our false ego. Centering has helped me become more aware of when I am coming from false ego and when I am coming from my greater Being, who is love.

Another important concept is discernment. My experience has been that my ability to discern what is right for me has greatly improved. Allowing parts of myself that I had "locked into closets," such as anger energy, back into myself has helped me enormously. Furthermore, all this "clearing" that so many of us are involved in obviously has some effect as well. The picture I am getting here is one of continually washing a window in order to see clearly. In general, working with my guides, and learning to be more grounded, in my body, and more "real," has all helped in my discernment.

If I am ever unsure about an issue, I first center myself and then I tune in. For example, I might tune into the energy of a workshop leader to help me discern if the seminar is right for me. Or, if I am debating whether to buy a certain book, I hold it in my hands and try to get a feel for whether this information is right for me. At times I get a nauseous feeling in my gut, even though the words sound nice, the cover is pretty, and the topic is supposedly enlightening.

Another example is information that I hear through what I call my "New Age Grapevine." When I get into contact with certain "news" or new techniques regarding ascension or personal growth, I often try to discern where this information is coming from. Even if the words sound wonderful, if the energy behind it is not right, then I don't "buy" it.

Words can be very deceiving and I am learning to look beyond appearances, biographies, degrees and smiles. In fact, my dog has practiced this kind of discernment all of her life and is much better than I at detecting disharmonious energies.

I remember seeing a story on television about a conman who married a wealthy woman for her money. When he first appeared "on the scene," the whole family thought he was just wonderful. In fact, the only one who did not like him was the cat, which was unusually hostile to the man. She, of course, reacted to his energy, which was not truthful.

A Centering Exercise

There are many books available that talk about centering and provide exercises. Certainly practices such as Tai Chi, yoga, meditation, walking in nature, and listening to peaceful music are all options.

I would like to share a centering exercise that has helped me to ground the energies coming through and facilitate my ascension process.

I usually do a simple exercise at home or in the middle of a walk in nature. My experience is that the more I practice getting and staying centered, the easier it gets (except for those major clearing times where lifetimes of "stuff" get thrown up). Before I describe the exercise, let me clarify that my words are only suggestions. Please follow your intuition and change the exercise in whatever way feels right for you.

Stand with your legs apart and your hands by your side. Voice lovingly (or silently) your intention: "I intend to be clear. I intend to be centered. I am clear. I am centered. I am healthy. I am happy." (Or whatever else you want to say).

Then I call in St. Francis, the Archangels, Mahatma, Melchior, Melchizedek and others. At times I invite everybody that is supporting my ascension process, and that of the Earth. I ask for only the highest light. I ask these Beings to help me to fulfill my purpose.

(By the way, getting help is not a sign of weakness. It is a feature of a new understanding of the idea of cocreation. We are all creating this mass ascension together. This is connected to the concept that what supports your growth or highest good also supports everybody else's growth and highest good. This is also the case with your guides; they benefit from your evolution and you benefit from theirs.)

Another picture I like is one of angels with little vacuum cleaners that suck up any low-density energy that is not needed anymore. This energy gets taken out of my body, or energy system, or environment, and then gets transformed back into the light—where it can create something beautiful. Often I affirm, "I release all energy that does not support my growth and ascension. I release all limiting beliefs." Then I thank all the light beings supporting me.

At some point I have a sense that my energy fields, my aura, my body, are now clear and clean. If you are not sure, *see* them strong, clear, and purified.

Again, I might say something such as, "I am clear. I am abundant. I am loved. I am healthy." At this point, I try to let the love of my friends in and I call on the Mahatma energy or Source or God. *I allow the love in*; then I often get a color usually pink, blue or gold. The colors you need might be different. I see the color coming from Source and higher levels of my Being, and it enters my body from the top. For me the color is also connected with taking in love, or aliveness, or clarity, or joy, or any other characteristics from my greater Being and my friends.

I bring the color down through my body into my feet and deep into the Earth. Then I bring energy up from the Earth and see myself receiving it from her. I bring her energy up through me and back up to Source. I usually set an intention that the "energy dance" between Earth and myself is for the highest good for both of us and supports us in fulfilling our highest potential.

Now, I bring down the energy again, and then bring it back up and down a couple of times. I intuit which is more important at the moment—bringing down the light or grounding myself. Often, when there is a lot of energy coming through our bodies, grounding is more important.

(Another note: As time speeds up and growth is accelerated, doing this simple exercise for just five minutes can have an enormous effect on your well-being. Furthermore it can "save" you from con-fused probable future paths that you might have taken from a less centered place.)

As with cleaning teeth, it is better to do a couple of five minute clearings throughout the day than, let us say, one hour once a month. For me it is now a habit, and when I take my dog for a walk, I stop at my "powerplace" by a pond, and it happens almost by itself.

As time goes by, I realize more and more how important a clear intention is. Since we create all the time from many levels of our Being, I believe the "trick" is not so much to work hard on manifestation but to keep our intention clear and to have a vision about what we want to happen. Here are St. Francis' comments on holding a vision.

St. Francis on Holding A Vision

Holding a vision is a wonderful technique. It needs to be done in cooperation with your greater Self, which includes your Higher Self and your Source connection. You need to be clear what you want, truly want, and then you need to project it. A healthy body, a healed Earth, healed bodies (physical, emotional, mental, spiritual) around you, clean air, abundance and freedom are all visions to be held.

Now, it is important to hold these visions in the "eternal now," and not project them into a distant future. See the Earth cleared now. Flood her etheric body with light now. See your bodies clean and clear now. Know it will be so because you, in cooperation with, or better said as, your I AM Presence, said so.

Know also that anything in alignment with Source will manifest easily and quickly. Believe it. It does, in fact, take more energy to manifest discord and disharmony. Since this is all around you on Earth, you can see the power of humanity to manifest.

Now manifest, visualize, and accept. This is where many err. They visualize, for example, a clean and healthy body and, at the same time, fight the one they have. They project light, and rather than allow what is to just be there and transform in the light, they deny it. So we suggest you visualize, for example, a healthy body and then *let it go*. Then later, if you need to cry or express feelings of frustration, do so. Accept your tears, accept your anger and frustration, and let this energy be transformed in the light you brought in, the light that you are. Also if you wish, you can give the tears or whatever to us, or your guides and angel friends.

We would like to say a word to those who feel their conditions do not improve. First of all, when you heal, you heal. Sometimes you see effects right away and sometimes you do not realize all the healing that took place until you are "on the other side."

Ascension is, in many ways, the ultimate healing. Now, for many of you, your bodies are having a hard time with the energies. As one lightworker asked us recently, "If this ascension is about healing, how come my body aches all the time?" Well, we hope our chapter on the body will help you get an idea of the enormous transmutation that is demanded from your physical vehicle.

Secondly, you are healing many levels, past lives, alternate realities and possibly other people's energy patterns as well—remember, we are all connected. Let us take the example of past lives: As you continue on this process of ascension, you will probably have more and more insights of past lives and lessons there.

If you had a lot of physical problems, including illnesses or abuses, your body might react to these. Tell your body that *it is safe now*. Tell your body that *it is healthy now*. This includes those of you who have, let us say, cancer, AIDS or other diseases. You see, sometimes the soul decides that creating an illness can be a "fast track" to learning all your lessons or clearing many lifetimes of fear, abuse, and trauma. Although we generally like to see you all happy, pain-free, and enjoying life, we do not question the wisdom of your soul.

Furthermore, once you leave this wonderful school called Earth, it will not be the outer creations that are of importance, but the lessons you have learned and the healing you have done for yourself and others. All this is not so clear on this planet of "con-fusion." Some of the things that looked like "bad luck" from a limited Earth perspective, are later seen as the great learning tools they really were. Know that whatever your struggles or difficulties, *our love is with all of you.*

Anina:

After Saint Francis' comments about the concept of vision, I felt the impulse to express my vision. After reading this maybe you want to join me and write down yours. I hold a vision of a world of kindness and acceptance. I hold a vision where anger, sadness, frustration, despair and other feelings are not denied but are lovingly held in the I AM Presence and the cosmic heart.

I hold a vision were beings are free and not tyrannized by others or by a time clock. I hold a vision were expression is easy and flows. I hold a vision where energy flows without resistance and there is no judgment. I hold a vision where we spontaneously say "no" to abuse and darkness and lovingly transmute such dense energies as they realize their own lightness. I hold a vision where there is no "right" or "wrong," but rather kindness and acceptance of "what is."

I hold a vision of Source energy and our vaster Self being deeply grounded in our bodies, which have completely turned to light. I hold a vision of joy coming back, and of no more denial. I hold a vision of anger flowing freely and letting us know exactly when to say "no." It will not even be called anger anymore. It will just be an energy "impulsing" us to say "no." No more denial.

I hold a vision of my Self as a co-creator in perfect alignment with Source. I hold a vision of truth and harmony. I hold a vision of a happy and healthy planet full of joy and life.

11
The Body

St. Francis:

[Recorded from a reading]

The body has its own consciousness, its own intelligence, and it has its own memory. The body is your vehicle here on Earth. In a sense, you are separate from it but in the ultimate sense there is no separation, because *all consciousness is one*.

The body is, of course, very involved in the ascension process. In fact, it is an essential part of the process, and cooperation and communication between the different bodies (physical, mental, emotional and spiritual) is important.

The body wants to be loved and you can see how, in this, it is not so different from the rest of creation. Creation—being love—wants to express that love and receive it.

Let us repeat: *The body wants to be loved.* It is that simple, really. *Creation is love. All of us are love. All things, energies, consciousness thrive on love.* It cannot be any different. Only illusion tells us otherwise.

Loving the body means being with it in a gentle manner. This means giving the body the space in the morning to stretch and relax from its nightly ventures. It is eating when the body wants food, not eating when the body is stressed and wants to be quiet and go within. The body knows how to nourish itself, how to love itself, how to make the heart beat, how to be still, how to move slowly or quickly. The body knows how to stand and how to drop into itself quietly, restfully, with grace. The body is *love*, just like you are. There is nothing in this universe that is not love because *All That Is is love.*

71

Question: But what about distorted bodies, crippled bodies, boils on the skin, bad smelling, painful, aching bodies?

Answer: *They are love,* we say, and gently and lovingly hold them in our energy. All life has purpose and so do "distorted bodies." Something is being played out by life, something is being expressed, learned, mirrored. The bodies of Chernobyl are a mirror for something, and not separate from the bodies on *Athletics Magazine"*(if there is such [amused]). All is connected. Nothing in this creation exists in isolation and we hold your bodies—if you let us—in our loving energy just like you would hold our body of energy. They are all the same—just vibrating at different levels.

As you reach out to the tree outside, by the window, it embraces you. *Love is all.*

Have mercy on your body. It is doing its best. Are there distortions? Of course. Your whole world is full of distortions, but be quiet, let your body move, stretch, and let it whisper to you. Communicate with each other. Support each other. Ascension is not done alone. It is done by constantly talking, listening and supporting, and loving each other. Your different levels of Self, your many bodies, your I AM Presence. Ascension is a multi-leveled affair. It is deep and simple.

Loving The Body

[From a channeling for myself]

Now, as always, acceptance is the crux of the matter and that is where your problem with vision comes in. How can you have a vision and not have it turned into non-acceptance of what is? Now, for you, in this culture, one of the problems is that there is non-acceptance all around you. A whole industry (advertising) plays on the belief that you are not whole now, and need to purchase this or that to feel better.

So let us get practical, very practical. Let us assume you have a stomach ache, and that you also have a vision of a body and an energy field that flows without interference and disease. How can you run these in parallel, and we are now talking to you specifically, knowing that other energies might prefer other methods?

Accept your body just the way it is. Put your healing hands on the area that feels painful, and you do that anyway, intuitively. Tell the body that it is all right. Wrap it in pink light through visualization. Give it fluids or herbs or whatever it needs, and your intuition can guide you on this. *Relax* your body. This is actually a step in *acceptance* and many people are afraid to relax because it brings up issues. Now, *let it go.*

At another time, and preferably when body and mind feel good and you are not "fighting" another condition, you can create your vision:

Visualize a lightbody, a body full of light and joy. Visualize your body lighting up and releasing low density energy *easily.* (It does not have to be traumatic.) Have fun while you do it.

If the body feels overwhelmed, and sometimes the body feels as if the impossible is demanded of it, *stop* and soothe the body. Explain the ascension process and how it includes the body, and that the body will feel lighter and more joyful. Say, "I accept you now, the way you are," to balance out any feelings of being rejected that your cells might have.

You can see that there are no exact recipes for how to do this. It is a process of communication with your body, and with your personality and your greater Self, including us. It is truly a co-operation, co-creation. So bathe your body in pink light and let us soothe it.

The body is not like the mind. It does not understand complicated concepts, although it carries out its functions beautifully and it certainly takes great intelligence to keep all those organs going and working in order. But the body lives in the *now*.

This is one of the big differences between the physical and the mental bodies. As the mind "re-members" a scary incident or gets engulfed in a movie, forgetting it is safe, the body will act as if all this is happening now. The body lives in the *now* or what it perceives as the *now*. So a body can tense up when seeing fire, remembering having being burned in a past life, even though it is now at a safe distance from the fire. Now, you say to us: "But that is living in the past." No it is not, because in the "relative now," so-called past lives happen simultaneously.

Now, as you know, we do not advise "digging up past lives." Aligning of your energy structure will automatically provide healing in whatever time sequence or dimension is required. In fact, being in slowed-down light allows you to heal all levels of Self, whether you know it or not.

So, when you talk to the body, talk to it in the *now*. Say literally: "You are safe *now*. God loves you *now*" or whatever else your Self impulses you to say.

Speak to your body. Your body is just as distraught about certain aspects of this ascension, as is the personality. Some of your cells are virtually afraid of dying. This is why we repeat that ascension is transformation of the body and not death of the body.

In the past, when Earth's vibration was lower, ascension did imply death of the physical vehicle. This is no longer true, unless you wish it to be so. But that is a decision between you and your Higher Self.

The body is an organization, if you will. Our channel is seeing the picture of an anthill—and yes, a well-functioning anthill with every ant-body knowing its function and purpose, and working with vigor and joy is a good analogy.

Now, a lot of the commands for running the body come from the brain, but some come from other sources. You know about the body continuing after the brain is declared dead. In fact, a soul can leave before a body dies, and a soul can enter and leave before a body is born. So bodies have their own karma. We do not like to use the word karma but you, in your cells, carry beliefs and energy patterns held by your great-great-grandparents. In this way, history is still alive in you. When we talk about history, we refer to mass beliefs and other environmental experiences of certain times. There are energies in your body right now that remember the plague for example. When we talk about the clearing of the body, these facts need to be considered. And again, we say the mind is overwhelmed when asked to figure out why any particular feeling, energy, or thought comes up. Its origins could be millions of years ago.

Now, as to past lives/parallel lives, your body is connected to all of your bodies and as you "en-lighten" this body, you enlighten the others as well. As you remember, for example, a hanging in a parallel life, your throat can be affected, in this moment, and your voice might go up as this memory gets activated. So what do you do?

As always, you do not worry. Stay in the now and love yourself and your body, wrapping it in pink, talking to it, touching it with love or letting it move, tone, or sound. From such treatment with love will come a relaxation, an allowing in of light and love, and that is really the easiest and most elegant way of healing that we know. Trust your body and Higher Self in cooperation to guide you. There need not be conflict.

Focus is important to the body. Lack of focus is a bit like getting into a car and starting it and saying, "Drive wherever you want"—anxiety-provoking and confusing for the car [amused]. Now, of course the car needs to be washed, maintained, and given some idle time, especially after overheating, but when you get into the driver's seat, you need to drive and take control.

Here is the word that so many of you hate. Controlling behavior has become a negative catch phrase but control is not bad. Being in control of your body is good. Now, you do not dominate the body and override its intelligence. When your back hurts, you do not say, "Oh, let's lift another heavy box." No, you cooperate; you talk to the body and honor its intelligence, but you do not let it control you.

Following the body means listening to the body, not surrendering to it. It is very anxiety-provoking to a body to be given control, as it is anxiety-provoking for a five-year-old child to be given control of a family.

When people control the body from their false ego and do not listen to its signals, then there is confusion. And, of course, creating from your false ego always results in confusion, regardless of the area of activity. So, as always, it is about listening to your Higher Self, Oversoul, and Source connection and then gently "aligning" the body.

You have seen pictures of bodies under total control and of bodies just doing what they feel like, the control center at times intoxicated or simply confused. Those are all extremes. The ideal of a "perfect" body is a harsh one, and a poor substitute for Self-love.

Let us say more about the body. The body needs to feel safe. This is how it relaxes. This is how it feels joy and well-being. How does it feel safe? It feels safe when it feels led, loved, appreciated, and taken care of.

Now, who leads the body? As the body grows up, it is mostly the mother who provides this sense of safety. It is also provided by the soul of the person, and his or her guides. Many children see their guides or at least sense their presence. The father also provides a sense of safety, but not like the mother since the child's body has spent approximately nine months inside the mother and has bonded with her body. Of course, if the mother leaves, or goes to work, the father can be a fine provider of comfort and safety, but there will be a transition and the body will always remember the mother as its home as it was growing.

Hating the baby inside, or stress for the mother while the embryo develops, will set a body up for tension, "nonrelaxation," and "dis-ease," as will, for example, a war in a country where the body lives. War has a devastating effect on each body's immune system. Of course, everything can be healed, and a lot of physical healing has to do with relaxation and a sense of safety. Soul can provide that, and so can Higher Self, and Source. Let it in.

Let us review: The body lives in the *now*. The body needs guidance. It needs to feel safe. The emotions and mental parts of the personality need to be balanced, since denied emotions and thoughts tend to express themselves by creating disease in the body.

Relaxation is a key, and love is the ultimate "healer." The body needs to be accepted just the way it is. A new vision of a "lighter" body needs to be created in parallel with, not in opposition, to the present body.

Past/parallel lives influence the body but *all* can be cleared *easily* with the new energies available. For those of you like our channel who are skeptical of this statement, treat it as an affirmation.

[From a reading]

In truth there is no death. Death does not exist. And what you call death, the crossing over into other realms, is not a "failure." Many beings decide to learn more on "the other side," and then choose to come back in a new body rather than try to "re-model" the old one. The Self decides, as always.

The body needs to feel appreciated and loved, and will perform "miracles" if treated this way—ascension, of course, being one of the greatest miracles.

Movement: the body needs to move; in fact, life is movement. If you are paralyzed, tap your fingers or move your eyes. Let the energy inside move you. Ask the body and Higher Self for guidance on when to move, how fast, and which parts. Many energies involved in the ascension process prefer low-impact movement but some, the "piccolo flutes" among you, like a faster pace.

Take some time with slow movement and go into your body and love each part of it. Wrap it in pink. After doing this, *let it go.* Do not think about it anymore. Do not create problems after the exercise such as, "Did I do it right? Did I love the body enough?"

[From another reading]

Food: allow yourself to eat. Don't beat up on yourself or your body for eating. Distance yourself from all this nonsense on your television and in your magazines about the "perfect" body. If you feel pulled in by the nonsense, say, "This does not apply to me."

Love your body the way it is. If you need to eat less, so be it, but at the same time love yourself exactly as you are at every moment. If a part of you feels pain around your appearance, love that part and then put it aside. Love as well the part that says, "I do not care how I look."

As all of these parts are expressed—possibly on paper, or in your mind—they will create a balance. The part that hates your appearance need not be killed. Love it. As long as it is in balance, it cannot hurt you. Love it and it will help you to look better without waging an emotional war within. Love it and it will relax.

So, love your body and also remember it is just your "suit." Once you are beyond Earth, you can choose any appearance you wish.

Anina:

Since the energy experiences associated with ascension started a couple of years ago, my body has sometimes reacted in strange ways. I have noticed that the body often needs reassurance that whatever is going on is okay. It seems to me that the body is very connected to the inner child. I have found it helpful to talk to my body and explain about the process of ascension and how it plays a major part in this endeavor.

I often tell my body that I am proud of how well it is doing and how well it now holds a higher frequency. I explain that it is playing a part in the Divine Plan and is fulfilling its function beautifully. I tell it not to worry about pains and aches, and that I and St. Francis, and our friends "on the other side," are all involved in this ascension project and are supporting it.

I have promised my body that it can express itself when it feels scared and overwhelmed. I then bring in St. Francis and other aspects of my greater Self, and they answer any questions and offer reassurance. I have promised my body that I will treat it gently and with love, and any health practitioner, massage therapist or other healer who does not do this is not allowed to work on my body. I have promised my body the movement it needs and the rest it needs. I have promised my body that I will support it in this process as it supports me.

I will give you some detailed examples of conversations between St. Francis and my body. In the beginning, it seemed a little silly to me to talk to my body or to hear St. Francis talk to my body, but after such talks I really feel better physically.

St. Francis: This is St. Francis. We would like to speak to the body.
Cells: Yes, we are here.
St. Francis: How are you?

Cells: Not good.
St. Francis: What is the problem?
Cells: Feeling overwhelmed. Everything seems too much. All these traumatic experiences are coming up.
St. Francis: You are safe *now*.
Cells: Really?
St. Francis: Yes, really. You are completely safe. Whatever comes through is just for clearing. You can let go of tension and constriction. Just *let it move through you*. We are always with you.
Cells: You will protect us?
St. Francis: Yes, yes, absolutely.
Cells: So, we can relax?
St. Francis: Yes. *Relax.*
Cells: Thank you.
St. Francis: You are very welcome. You are doing tremendous work, important work. You are pioneers.
Cells: Really?
St. Francis: Yes, and you have the full support of numerous lightbeings.
Cells: Well, we've got a sense of that.
St. Francis: Good. Very good.
Cells: Thank you.
St. Francis: You are very loved; very loved and very much appreciated.
Cells: We feel more relaxed now.
St. Francis: Good.

Or on another occasion:
St. Francis: Good morning, cells.
Cells: Good morning.
St. Francis: How are you?
Cells: Tired.
St. Francis: You are all doing very well. Very well.
Cells: Really? The personality does not think so.
St. Francis: Well, at times she gets confused.

Cells: Thank you.

St. Francis: You know what we mean. She has never done this particular type of ascension, so, she gets impatient, or rather really afraid, and sometimes she falls back into blaming somebody.

Cells: Usually this body—us.

St. Francis: But she is trying, isn't she?

Cells: Yes, that's true.

St. Francis: Cut her some slack.

Cells: Okay.

St. Francis: You, as cells, know you are good, don't you?

Cells: Sometimes we wonder.

St. Francis: Because of blame?

Cells: Yes.

St. Francis: Blame, fear—all that is false. Ignore it.

Cells: Ignore it?

St. Francis: Yes, offer it to us, we will take any blame and fear energy and transmute it into light.

Cells: We do not have to carry it anymore?

St. Francis: You are coming to a point where you *cannot* carry it anymore. Remember our—all of us, Higher Self, other parts of Self, personality, you the body—objective is to go into light.

Cells: Right.

St. Francis: You cannot carry fear and blame into light.

Cells: You cannot?

St. Francis: No, so let it go.

Cells: Okay, we will give it to you.

St. Francis: Yes, give it to us or our angel friends, the ones who the personality sees as little "energy dustbusters" with vacuums. That is a good image. It is the idea of transmutation.

Cells: Can we let it go right now?

St. Francis: Yes. Release all fear, blame, anger, frustration or any other energy not needed anymore. Let it be sucked up into the vacuums held by angels. Let it be transformed.

Cells: Okay.
St. Francis: Okay. We love you and send you some pink light.
Cells: Thank you.
St. Francis: You are welcome.

For me, communicating with the body is an ongoing process and the more I do it, the more I understand its importance. St. Francis has told me that the body—just as my subpersonalities or other energies of my being—needs to express what is going on. Somehow there is something very healing about expression, especially if it is received by a loving audience. St. Francis told me that, in general, I do not have to "problem solve" for my body.

"Your cells know very well how to make the heart beat," he once commented laughingly. And then he said, "Trust your body and talk to it. That is part of loving it, and, after all, it is love that is most important here."

12

Brian Grattan

Anina:

After hearing about Brian Grattan, I soon got in touch with the energy that he channeled. I became very excited and registered for his Easter seminar in Basel, Switzerland.

A couple of days later, I started doubting. My conditioning of unworthiness and "not good enough" came up. I could sense Brian's high frequency and my ego began telling me that I did not belong in that seminar. Part of me was sure that Brian and other people in the group would find out who I really was: "Bad and not really worthy to be with them." At one point, this part of me considered canceling the seminar. That night I had the following dream:

I was at the seminar in Basel. There were other people around who seemed to ignore me. I got scared, and feelings of rejection surfaced. Then Brian walked over from the other side of the room and looked straight at me. He said, "You are not afraid of me. You are afraid of your Self."

I woke up from the dream and knew immediately what he meant. The "Self" that he embodied and talked about was also my "Self." By pretending that he (and others) were worth more than me or better than me, I was denying my own Self, my own divinity, and also my own power.

I finally went to Basel, and part of me questioned my sanity regarding my decision to make such a long trip for a five-day seminar, but something (or someone) pushed me.

At the seminar, we did a lot of energy work, mainly using visualizations and toning. Brian repeatedly commented at the workshop that it was *the group* that was "defining the terms," *the group* that was creating this new, "light-filled" reality.

One night, I dreamed that all of us were in a big auditorium and were working with energy and toning. It was one of these dream/experiences that I sometimes have. The auditorium looked a little different than the one we had used during the day. The next morning, Brian said that he had wanted to sleep, but *the group* had decided to work at night. I knew what he meant.

The main theme of the visualizations was about bringing in the light and anchoring it into Earth and our bodies. It was all about raising frequency, Self-healing, and clearing. In many meditations we visualized parts of Earth being cleared and Brian continued to comment on other Beings helping us.

In one visualization, he talked about one of various Councils of Twelve. These are groups of highly-evolved Beings and I felt their love and their appreciation for our work on Earth. At one point I saw them (with my inner eyes) bowing to us in gratitude. Part of me found this hard to believe, and I decided later that I had probably imagined this picture. After the exercise, Brian said that the members of the Council of Twelve had actually bowed to us in gratitude. At that point, I started crying and took in the feeling of being loved and appreciated by Beings who understood our work.

On Easter Monday, Brian died, but walking around Basel the next day, I felt his energy everywhere.

Back home I had a series of dreams connected with him and I want to share a couple that were especially helpful to me.

One of the dreams was again about the issue of what I call Self-authority. In the dream, I was in my parents' house, where I grew up. Brian was doing a retreat there. As the seminar ended, we were given the opportunity to ask questions. I thought, "Well, even if I ask Brian a question, I am still the one who has to solve whatever problem there is by myself." As I thought that, I suddenly could feel all this love from Brian permeating my house. I got it. I need to solve my life issues myself but I am not alone. We are never alone.

Another dream was at a time when I was going through a period of frustration. I wondered what my real purpose was and if I was really part of something or just a rather "useless" member of society. I cried out to my soul, "What is my purpose? What is my purpose?"

I had the following dream: I was in the countryside digging trenches. I looked up and noticed Brian. Suddenly I felt all this love and compassion for humanity. It was an incredible and very sweet feeling.

As I awoke, I heard the words, "new pathways." That made a lot of sense to me. My hope is that through my books, conversations with friends, and just plain thinking of new and more unlimited thoughts, I am, in some small way, contributing to the raising of consciousness and the creation of a new reality.

Another dream came a couple of months after the seminar in Basel. I dreamed I was a monk in a brown cloak. I was standing upright with my arms stretched to the heavens. A voice said, "Now that you have received St. Francis, it is time to receive *the Father*."

The next morning after breakfast, I randomly opened Brian's book. The first words I saw were, "Mahatma (the Father)."

My communion with the Mahatma energy continues. I feel very much connected with all those lightworkers who knowingly or unknowingly work with this energy, or any other energy that is connected with Source. Let me also add that the Mahatma energy is not just male. It is in fact male and female, and now perfectly balanced.

In closing I would like to say that I did not know Brian, the personality, very well, but I certainly know and am connected to the energy he represented. I thank him, not just for embodying this great energy so beautifully, but also for being so human and for sharing his own struggles with the ascension process.

13

Idolization

Anina:

Why do we idolize? Why do we give our power away? Sometimes it is so subtle that it takes some time to understand what has happened. Sometimes we do it on a national level, an extreme example being the German Reich in the 1930's and the people's love/hate relationship to their Fuhrer.

One day I asked St. Francis about the topic of idolization.

St Francis:

Idolization is an interesting subject, isn't it? So there is an "idolizer" and a person being "idolized," and you have experienced both sides of the coin.

Now, feeling a certain admiration for another's achievement or work is normal and need not be feared. Where it does get "sticky" is when comparison comes in, as in, "Oh, I could never do this." And then there are feelings of inequality and the personality begins thinking, "Oh, they must be better than I am. They are more worthy than I am."

Ultimately, such expressions are the "logical" extensions of a sense of unworthiness. A person who feels truly worthy will not put another over or under Self. He or she will enjoy learning certain skills or tricks from a mentor or teacher, but will not see that person as better or more worthy, or less worthy for that matter.

True Self-esteem comes from knowing Self and knowing one's divinity—which is no different from our divinity, Jesus' divinity or Source itself, because ultimately we are all Source. True Self-esteem comes from the connection with your I AM Presence, your Source connection.

Idolizing is really a waste of time and puts the responsibility of Self-awareness and growth on another. This never, never works.

You are "respons-able" for your own growth, your own life, your belief systems, and your energy structure. As we have explained before, this does not mean that you have to do it alone. At some point you will understand that the idea of being alone and "struggling" alone is quite illusory. At some point you will understand more clearly how everything in creation is really a group effort, and how you are part of a big tapestry of energies all focused on growth and new learning, or enlightenment if you want to use that word. Nobody is alone. So, you are free to ask for help and support from the universe *and* you are "respons-able."

Now, rather than see this respons-ability as a burden, we suggest that you can change this point view and put respons-ability more in the category of excitement, joy and fulfillment. *You have the ability to create and play around with different building blocks.* Remember how much fun you had with those as a baby, before it all became so burdensome and overwhelming? *Free yourself,* and go one step at a time, and know that you are not alone.

Last but not least, let us remind you that the part of oneself that likes to idolize others, or oneself, need not be killed. It is again about expressing this part, through writing for example, and accepting it. Whatever you are aware of cannot sabotage you. As always, it is about bringing all denied parts into awareness rather than playing them out in some unconscious manner and creating chaos. *Intend to be clear.*

14

Compassion

St. Francis:

So, what is compassion? It is not taking care of others necessarily, unless that is the appropriate response at the time. It is not being "nice," unless that is an appropriate response at the time. It can mean being firm and loving. It can involve saying "no" or saying "yes." So you see, compassion is not a behavior. It is a state that originates from within. Compassion and love come from within. Let us repeat: compassion and love come from within.

"So how do you express it?" our channel asks, jumping ahead here.

Please, for a moment, let us go very slowly. First of all, you do not express compassion. Compassion is a state, not a behavior. Secondly, when you are love or, more appropriately, remember that you are love—and do not get confused by our little friend the ego—then *compassion will express itself naturally, without being forced.* You see, it is natural to express compassion or, more accurately, it is natural to be a vessel *and* to be one filled with love and compassion.

It is unnatural not to feel and not to cry when another suffers. It is not natural to have a "stiff upper lip," just as it is not natural to constantly get swept away by the emotional body. Now, there is no criticism in our description. Our "hairy, little friend," the ego has thrown enough mud in everybody's direction that at times it is hard to see clearly.

Let us continue. We are giving our channel the picture of a luminous egg shining through a big crusting of mud which surrounds it. That is another way of looking at who you all are—Light. As your light increases, the mud will automatically fall off. Your love will shine out and you will see more clearly and be more able to make intelligent choices. Sometimes compassion can be tricky. Your ego tells you to "help" somebody while your stomach revolts. If that happens, stop and look at your intention. Are you giving out of love or out of guilt? A "should" is a good indication that there is guilt. Remember, your intent determines what you create. Even if you "do good," if it comes from a place of guilt, you will ultimately create more guilt.

Many people give from a sense of "being bad." "I am bad so I will help others. That will make me a better person." Please remember that love comes from within. Trying to "fix" oneself from without will not work.

This is the reason why so many well-meaning projects backfire. They do not come from a place of love and clarity but from "con-fusion."

Having said this, let us add that there is, of course, no "perfect giving," just as there is no "perfect parenting" or "perfect anything" [amused]. This is a plane of learning, and trial and error is one of the ways to do so. It is much better to make mistakes and get back up than to close off your heart until you see yourself as "good enough" to give. So relax. The universe is supporting you in your evolution. All of us are. Even your "mean neighbor" on a higher level is supporting you. In fact, on some level of your Beings, you are having a blast about your squabbles and see the lighter side of this "Earth drama."

15

Connection And Co-Creation

Anina:

I believe connection and co-creation are concepts we will become more aware of in the near future. I feel that I will receive more information on these topics when the time is right.

The fact that my insights depend on other people's insights and awareness is a good example of how we are all connected and influence each other. If my neighbor understands something that I do not understand, he or she will help me gain new insight on that particular subject. This is true even if we never talk to each other. I believe that insights, revelations, or "relative truths" have an energy of their own which is being communicated by simply being there.

This is not to say that it would not be fun to talk to my neighbor about a subject, but it is also important to acknowledge the power of thoughts and the power of the new vibrations that we all experience on this planet. I believe that part of the reason for the new awakening interest in energy, healing, ecology, spirituality, and other such subjects, is that vibrations have been greatly accelerated.

St. Francis:

There is a saying that "man is a social animal." Support or rejection from others surely influences behavior and feelings.

Some refer to the "web of life" to describe the idea that all life is connected. It is a helpful metaphor as long as one can keep in mind that life is much more than a three-dimensional reality. There are other dimensions, realities, and probabilities all going on at the same time, and they are all nurtured and influenced by each other. A pebble thrown into a pond is not only felt on other continents but also in other realities.

Similarly, any change in belief systems affects consciousness everywhere. Human beings, animals, plants, and rocks for that matter, are not isolated consciousnesses floating around in some empty space. Whatever decisions and choices are followed through by one consciousness affect many different consciousnesses and many different realities.

Other consciousnesses can, for example, affect the state of mind and physical well-being of a person. Our channel clearly feels the uplifting and refreshing effect of an ocean shore or, for that matter, a piece of music played and enjoyed in the privacy of her home. It is really all about consciousnesses intermingling with each other, changing each other.

[Excerpt from a reading to a lightworker who asked about organizing a workshop.]

As you have already noticed, it is not always easy to be on the physical plane. The sheer details which are part of the physical can at times feel overwhelming. Please remember that the universe is supporting you. This is a co-creation, and you do not need to do it alone. Let go of "false responsibility" and ask when you need assistance. Ask the universe for help to type your newsletter. Ask the universe for money when needed. Ask and you shall be given. Only when you insist on doing it alone is it hard for the universe to give.

Know that your work is supported and greatly appreciated by all of us. Like a boat on a river, you are not asked to move by yourself. You are asked to stay "in the flow," as this is the easiest and fastest way to get to our goal (and we mean you, ourselves, and all here).

16

The Mass Ascension Plan

Anina:

The only certain thing about "the plan" seems to be that it is forever changing.

I am also sure that many intelligences and energies are working with love, patience and commitment on supporting Earth's and our mass ascension. This little planet will not be destroyed. I feel that very deeply.

However, how gentle and easy the transition to the higher dimensions will be is up to all of us. How much are we going to love ourselves and the Earth? How gentle, courageous, and honest are we going to be when our "demons" come up? Are we going to suppress this energy or will we let it be healed by the light? And very practically, will we take time to not only recycle but also reuse? Will we find time to hug our loved ones? Will we be courageous and follow our truth rather than learned "shoulds" and old conditioning? Will we hold Earth in love while she goes through her clearing?

Can we continue to hold a vision of love while not denying those aspects of ourselves that feel hurt, wounded or afraid? We must not put these aspects into the driver's seat of our lives. Rather, we need to expose them to the light, to healing.

I believe our choices in regard to all these questions will affect Earth, and which future probabilities will be chosen by Earth and by all on the planet.

Since everything is connected, all of us have a part to play and everybody counts. We can all work on forgiving ourselves, forgiving others, sending love to Earth, sending love to others. There is always something we can do through our thoughts, which have reality.

Since all of us are involved in the co-creation of this new reality, how could anybody know the final outcome? Yes, our guides can tell us about probabilities and likely outcomes, but what will actually happen is up to us—to humanity and all the other energies affecting Earth, including animals, plants, and other intelligences, such as our guides.

I believe we can all learn to love ourselves and others and our Earth more, and we *can* create a gentle and loving transition into the higher frequencies. And if it gets "rocky" for a while, we can survive that, too. For we are not just the little personalities that we see with our physical eyes. We are all powerful, spiritual Beings.

I would like to close with another dream. After I finished the first draft of this book I had the following dream.

In the dream, somebody asks, "Do you want to see the future?"

"Yes," I say, "but I do not want to see future probabilities of doom and gloom. I want to see the future probability where our project (mass ascension) is successful."

The dream changes and I experience myself flying around within a city (like a superman, or rather superwoman). I see beautiful buildings with huge windows and big plants inside. In fact, inside and outside seem in harmony. Next, I see a couple of people and they smile at me. Everybody seems happy and the smiles are authentic and innocent. People seem "lighter" and do not carry all the pain that we now carry. I realize that they do not carry the past the way we do now.

I wake up and feel happy. I say "thank you" to whoever co-created this dream with me. I now have more of a feel of the vision that we are all creating together.

About the Author

Born in Germany in 1961, Anina grew up in a quiet village near Munich. In college she studied Business both in Germany and England. After several years in the business world, she met her husband who is American.

They moved to the United States where Anina completed an MA in Counseling Psychology. After several years of working as a therapist and supervisor, her channeling and energy experiences started full force. Anina was then guided to focus her efforts on writing, channeling and integrating the new energies.

At present, she lives in a small town in the country where she enjoys a quiet and simple life. She spends most of her time writing and meditating.

CATALOG REQUESTS & BOOK ORDERS

Catalogs will gladly be sent upon request. Simply call the number below, or visit our on-line Internet bookstore at the web site below.

Book orders must be prepaid: check, money order, international coupon, VISA, MasterCard, Discover Card, and American Express accepted.

To place your order, call toll-free, fax, or mail to:

OUGHTEN HOUSE PUBLICATIONS

PO Box 2008

LIVERMORE · CALIFORNIA · 94551-2008 · USA

PHONE: (510) 447-2332

TOLL-FREE: 1-888-ORDERIT

FAX: (510) 447-2376

E-MAIL: oughtenhouse.com

INTERNET: www.oughtenhouse.com